AQA Science
Additional Science

Revision Guide

New GCSE

Pauline Anning
Niva Miles
John Scottow

Series Editor
Lawrie Ryan

Nelson Thornes

AQA examination questions are reproduced by permission of the
Assessment and Qualifications Alliance.

Published in 2011 by:
Nelson Thornes Ltd
Delta Place
27 Bath Road
CHELTENHAM
GL53 7TH
United Kingdom

11 12 13 14 15 / 10 9 8 7 6 5 4 3 2 1

A catalogue record for this book is available from the British Library

ISBN 978 1 4085 0843 5

Cover photograph: Jack Peters/Getty Images

Page make-up by Wearset Ltd, Boldon, Tyne and Wear

Printed and bound in Spain by GraphyCems

Photo acknowledgements
Page 1 Martyn F. Chillmaid; B2.1.5 Eric Grave/Science Photo Library;
B2.2.1 Cordelia Molloy/Science Photo Library; B2.2.4 Noel Hendrickson/
Getty; B2.3.1 J.C. Revy, ISM/Science Photo Library; B2.3.5 iStockphoto;
B2.4.3 iStockphoto; B2.6.1 Corel 706 (NT); C2.2.5a Alamy/Rob Walls;
C2.2.5b Innershadows/Fotolia; C2.2.6 Pasieka/Science Photo Library;
C2.3.3 Bloomberg/Getty Images; C2.3.6 Sciencephotos/Alamy;
C2.4.9a Martyn F. Chillmaid; C2.4.9b Fuse/Getty Images; P2.2.7 iStockphoto;
P2.3.5 AFP/Getty Images; P2.3.7 Fstop/Getty Images; P2.5.2 iStockphoto;
P2.5.3 Fotolia; P2.5.4 Cordelia Molloy/Science Photo Library; P2.7.4 NASA/
NOAO/AURA/NSF/T. Rector and B.A. Wolpa.

Additional Science

Contents

Welcome to AQA GCSE Science!   **1**

B2 Unit 2 Biology   **2**

1   Cells, tissues and organs   **2**
1.1   Animal and plant cells   2
1.2   Bacteria and yeast   2
1.3   Specialised cells   3
1.4   Diffusion   3
1.5   Tissues and organs   4
1.6   Organ systems   4
End of chapter questions   5

2   Organisms in the environment   **6**
2.1   Photosynthesis   6
2.2   Limiting factors   6
2.3   How plants use glucose   7
2.4   Making the most of photosynthesis   8
2.5   Organisms in their environment   8
2.6   Measuring the distribution of organisms   9
2.7   How valid is the data?   10
End of chapter questions   11

3   Enzymes   **12**
3.1   Proteins, catalysts and enzymes   12
3.2   Factors affecting enzyme action   12
3.3   Enzymes in digestion   13
3.4   Speeding up digestion   13
3.5   Making use of enzymes   14
3.6   High-tech enzymes   14
End of chapter questions   15

4   Energy from respiration   **16**
4.1   Aerobic respiration   16
4.2   The effect of exercise on the body   16
4.3   Anaerobic respiration   17
End of chapter questions   18

5   Simple inheritance in animals and plants   **19**
5.1   Cell division and growth   19
5.2   Cell division in sexual reproduction   20
5.3   Stem cells   21
5.4   From Mendel to DNA   21
5.5   Inheritance in action   22
5.6   Inherited conditions in humans   23
5.7   Stem cells and embryos – science and ethics   24
End of chapter questions   25

6   Old and new species   **26**
6.1   The origins of life on Earth   26
6.2   Exploring the fossil evidence   27
6.3   More about extinction   27
6.4   Isolation and the evolution of new species   28
End of chapter questions   29

Examination-style questions   **30**

C2 Unit 2 Chemistry   **32**

1   Structure and bonding   **32**
1.1   Chemical bonding   32
1.2   Ionic bonding   32
1.3   Formulae of ionic compounds   33
1.4   Covalent bonding   34
1.5   Metals   34
End of chapter questions   35

2   Structure and properties   **36**
2.1   Giant ionic structures   36
2.2   Simple molecules   36
2.3   Giant covalent structures   37
2.4   Giant metallic structures   38
2.5   The properties of polymers   38
2.6   Nanoscience   39
End of chapter questions   40

3   How much?   **41**
3.1   The mass of atoms   41
3.2   Masses of atoms and moles   42
3.3   Percentages and formulae   43
3.4   Equations and calculations   44
3.5   The yield of a chemical reaction   44
3.6   Reversible reactions   45
3.7   Analysing substances   46
3.8   Instrumental analysis   46
End of chapter questions   47

4   Rates and energy   **48**
4.1   How fast?   48
4.2   Collision theory and surface area   48
4.3   The effect of temperature   49
4.4   The effect of concentration or pressure   50
4.5   The effect of catalysts   50
4.6   Catalysts in action   51
4.7   Exothermic and endothermic reactions   51
4.8   Energy and reversible reactions   52
4.9   Using energy transfers from reactions   52
End of chapter questions   53

5   Salts and electrolysis   54
5.1   Acids and alkalis   54
5.2   Making salts from metals or bases   54
5.3   Making salts from solutions   55
5.4   Electrolysis   56
5.5   Changes at the electrodes   56
5.6   The extraction of aluminium   57
5.7   Electrolysis of brine   58
5.8   Electroplating   58
End of chapter questions   59

Examination-style questions   60

P2 Unit 2 Physics   62

1   Motion   62
1.1   Distance–time graphs   62
1.2   Velocity and acceleration   62
1.3   More about velocity–time graphs   63
1.4   Using graphs   63
End of chapter questions   64

2   Forces   65
2.1   Forces between objects   65
2.2   Resultant force   65
2.3   Force and acceleration   66
2.4   On the road   66
2.5   Falling objects   67
2.6   Stretching and squashing   68
2.7   Force and speed issues   69
End of chapter questions   70

3   Work, energy and momentum   71
3.1   Energy and work   71
3.2   Gravitational potential energy   71
3.3   Kinetic energy   72
3.4   Momentum   72
3.5   Explosions   73
3.6   Impact forces   73
3.7   Car safety   74
End of chapter questions   75

4   Current electricity   76
4.1   Electrical charges   76
4.2   Electric circuits   76
4.3   Resistance   77
4.4   More current–potential difference graphs   78
4.5   Series circuits   78
4.6   Parallel circuits   79
End of chapter questions   80

5   Mains electricity   81
5.1   Alternating current   81
5.2   Cables and plugs   82
5.3   Fuses   83
5.4   Electrical power and potential difference   84
5.5   Electrical energy and charge   85
5.6   Electrical issues   85
End of chapter questions   86

6   Radioactivity   87
6.1   Observing nuclear radiation   87
6.2   The discovery of the nucleus   87
6.3   Nuclear reactions   88
6.4   More about alpha, beta and gamma radiation   89
6.5   Half-life   90
6.6   Radioactivity at work   90
End of chapter questions   91

7   Energy from the nucleus   92
7.1   Nuclear fission   92
7.2   Nuclear fusion   93
7.3   Nuclear issues   93
7.4   The early universe   94
7.5   The life history of a star   95
7.6   How the chemical elements formed   96
End of chapter questions   97

Examination-style questions   98

Answers   100

Glossary   106

Welcome to AQA GCSE Science!

Key points

At the start of each topic are the important points that you must remember.

Maths skills

This feature highlights the maths skills that you will need for your Science exams with short, visual explanations.

This book has been written for you by the people who will be marking your exams, very experienced teachers and subject experts. It covers everything you need to revise for your exams and is packed full of features to help you achieve the very best that you can.

Key words are highlighted in the text and are shown **like this**. You can look them up in the glossary at the back of the book if you're not sure what they mean.

Where you see this icon, you will know that this topic involves How Science Works – a really important part of your GCSE.

IIII➤ *These questions check that you understand what you're learning as you go along. The answers are all at the back of the book.*

Many diagrams are as important for you to learn as the text, so make sure you revise them carefully.

Anything in the Higher boxes must be learned by those sitting the Higher Tier exam. If you're sitting the Foundation Tier, these boxes can be missed out.

The same is true for any other places that are marked [**H**].

Higher

AQA *Examiner's tip*

AQA Examiner's tips are hints from the examiners who will mark your exams, giving you important advice on things to remember and what to watch out for.

Bump up your grade

How you can improve your grade – this feature shows you where additional marks can be gained.

At the end of each chapter you will find:

End of chapter questions

These questions will test you on what you have learned throughout the whole chapter, helping you to work out what you have understood and where you need to go back and revise.

And at the end of each unit you will find:

AQA Examination-style questions

These questions are examples of the types of questions you will answer in your actual GCSE, so you can get lots of practice during your course.

You can find answers to the End of chapter and AQA Examination-style questions at the back of the book.

Key points

- Most human cells, like most animal cells, contain a nucleus, cytoplasm, cell membrane, mitochondria and ribosomes.
- Plant and algal cells contain everything in an animal cell, plus many also contain chloroplasts and a permanent vacuole filled with sap.
- Plant cells are different from animal cells because they have different functions.

1.1 Animal and plant cells

All living things are made of cells. Cells are small and can only be seen with microscopes. Light microscopes are used in schools. Electron microscopes magnify things thousands of times larger.

Most cells have some structures in common. They have:

- a **nucleus** to control the cell's activities
- **cytoplasm** where many chemical reactions take place
- a **cell membrane** that controls the movement of materials in and out of the cell
- **mitochondria** where energy is released during aerobic respiration
- **ribosomes** where **protein synthesis** takes place.

▐▐▶ **1** *In which part of the cell is energy released during respiration?*

Plant and **algal cells** also have:

- a rigid **cell wall** made of **cellulose** for support
- **chloroplasts** that contain **chlorophyll** for photosynthesis; the chloroplasts absorb light energy to make food
- a **permanent vacuole** containing cell sap.

Algae are simple aquatic organisms which have many features similar to plant cells.

Key words: nucleus, cytoplasm, cell membrane, mitochondria, ribosome, protein synthesis, algal cell, cell wall, cellulose, chloroplast, chlorophyll, permanent vacuole

Key points

- Bacteria are much smaller than plant and animal cells.
- Yeast is a single-celled organism, which is different from animal and plant cells.

AQA Examiner's tip

Make sure you can identify the differences between animal cells, plant cells, bacteria and yeast by looking at their features.

1.2 Bacteria and yeast

- Bacteria are very small and can only be seen with a powerful microscope.
- Bacterial cells have a cell membrane and a cell wall which surround cytoplasm.
- Bacteria do not have a nucleus so the **genetic material** is in the cytoplasm.
- When bacteria multiply they form a colony. **Bacterial colonies** can be seen with the naked eye.

▐▐▶ **1** *Why is it possible to see a bacterial colony but not a single bacterium?*

- Yeast is a single-celled organism.
- Yeast cells have a nucleus, cytoplasm and a membrane surrounded by a cell wall.

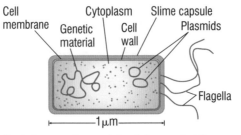

Bacteria come in a variety of shapes, but they all have the same basic structure

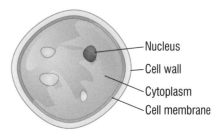

Yeast cells – these microscopic organisms have been useful to us for centuries

Key words: genetic material, bacterial colony

Student Book
pages 6–7

B2

1.3 Specialised cells

Student Book
pages 8–9

B2

Key points

- There are many different types of cell.
- Cells are specialised to carry out a particular function, e.g. fat cells, cone cells, root hair cells and sperm cells.
- The structure of a cell gives a clue to its function.

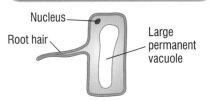

A root hair cell

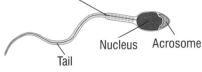

A sperm cell

There are many types of animal and plant cell. As an organism matures, each cell develops into a particular type. The structure of the cell is linked to its function:

- If a cell has many mitochondria it must need a lot of energy, e.g. muscle cell, sperm cell.
- If a cell has many ribosomes it is making a lot of protein, e.g. gland cells which produce enzymes.
- Cells with tails are able to move, e.g. sperm cells.
- Receptor cells have special structures which enable them to detect stimuli, e.g. the cone cells in the eye are light sensitive.
- Neurons are **specialised** to carry impulses from receptors to the CNS.
- Plant cells with many chloroplasts will be photosynthesising, e.g. mesophyll cells of a leaf.
- Root hair cells increase the surface area of the root so that it can absorb water and mineral ions efficiently.

▐▶ **1** *Why do muscle cells need a lot of mitochondria?*

AQA *Examiner's tip*

Do not be put off if you are asked to suggest a function for an unfamiliar cell. Look at the structures in the cell for clues.

Key word: specialised

1.4 Diffusion

- Molecules in gases and liquids move around randomly because of the energy they have.
- **Diffusion** is the spreading out of the particles of a gas, or of any substance in solution.
- The **net movement** into or out of cells depends on the concentration of the particles on each side of the cell membrane.
- Because the particles move randomly, there will be a net (overall) movement from an area of *high concentration* to an area of *lower concentration*.
- The difference in concentration between two areas is called the **concentration gradient.**
- The larger the difference in concentration, the faster the rate of diffusion.

▐▶ **1** *What determines the net movement of particles across a cell membrane?*

Key points

- Dissolved substances and gases can move into and out of cells by diffusion.
- Diffusion occurs more rapidly when there is a larger difference in concentration.

Both types of particles can pass through this membrane – it is freely permeable

Steep concentration gradient

Shallow concentration gradient

Three blue particles have moved from left to right by diffusion

Four blue particles have moved from left to right – but two have moved from right to left – a *net* movement of *two* particles to the right by diffusion

Examples are:

- the diffusion of oxygen into the cells of the body from the bloodstream as the cells are respiring (and using up oxygen)
- the diffusion of carbon dioxide into actively photosynthesising plant cells
- the diffusion of simple sugars and **amino acids** from the gut through cell membranes.

Key words: diffusion, net movement, concentration gradient, amino acid

Student Book
pages 10–11

B2

1.5 Tissues and organs

Key points

- A tissue is a group of cells with similar structure and function.
- Organs are made of several tissue types.

AQA Examiner's tip

Learn the levels of complexity in multicellular organisms:

cell → tissue → organ → system → whole body

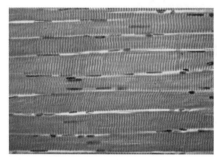

Muscle tissue like this contracts to move your skeleton

Tissues

During the development of **multicellular organisms** the cells **differentiate**. Different cells have different functions. A tissue is a group of cells with similar structure and function. Animal tissues include:

- **muscle tissue,** which can contract to bring about movement
- **glandular tissue,** to produce substances such as enzymes or hormones
- **epithelial tissue,** which covers some parts of the body.

⏵ 1 *What does glandular tissue produce?*

Plant tissues include:

- **epidermal tissue,** which covers the plant
- **mesophyll,** which can photosynthesise
- **xylem** and **phloem,** which transport substances around the plant.

Organs

Organs are made of tissues. The stomach is an organ made of:

- muscular tissue to churn the stomach contents
- glandular tissue to produce **digestive juices**
- epithelial tissue to cover the outside and the inside of the stomach.

The leaf, stem and root are plant organs which contain epidermal tissue, mesophyll, xylem and phloem.

- Groups of organs form **organ systems** to perform a particular function.
- The digestive system has several organs, including the **small intestine**.

Key words: multicellular organism, differentiate, muscle tissue, glandular tissue, epithelial tissue, epidermal tissue, mesophyll, xylem, phloem, digestive juice, organ system, small intestine

Student Book
pages 12–13

B2

1.6 Organ systems

Key points

- Groups of organs work together in an organ system.
- The digestive system in humans is adapted to exchange substances with the environment.
- Plant organs include stems, roots and leaves.

Bump up your grade

To avoid losing marks, make sure you know all the key words in this chapter. These biological terms are important for most of the topics in the unit.

The food you eat must be changed from **insoluble molecules** into soluble molecules. Only then can the soluble molecules be absorbed into the blood. The digestive system is responsible for this process.

The **digestive system** is a muscular tube which includes:

- glands, such as the pancreas and **salivary glands** which produce digestive juices
- the stomach and small intestine where digestion occurs
- the liver which produces bile
- the small intestine where the absorption of soluble food occurs
- the large intestine where water is absorbed from the undigested food, producing faeces.

⏵ 1 *Where is soluble food absorbed?*

Key words: insoluble molecule, digestive system, salivary gland

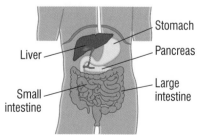

The organs of the digestive system work together to digest and absorb your food

1 List the structures which are found in both animal and plant cells.

Mitrochondria

2 Give three features of a plant or algal cell which are not found in animal cells.

Permanent vacuole, Chloroplasts, Cell wall

3 Where do most chemical reactions take place in a cell?

4 Name three organs in the human digestive system.

5 What chemical produced by the liver aids digestion?

6 Give two differences between a plant leaf cell and a yeast cell.

7 When, and in which direction, will diffusion take place in solutions and in gases?

8 What is meant by the term 'differentiation of cells'?

9 How is a leaf cell adapted to carry out photosynthesis?

10 Describe in detail what happens to food as it passes through the digestive system.

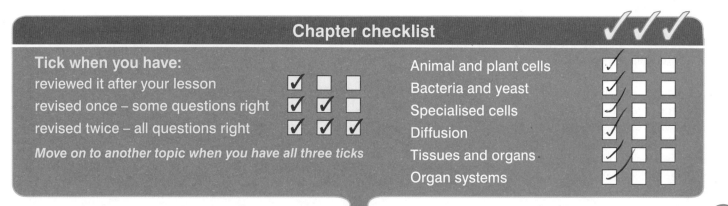

Chapter checklist ✓ ✓ ✓

Tick when you have:

reviewed it after your lesson	✓	□	□	Animal and plant cells	✓	□	□
revised once – some questions right	✓	✓	□	Bacteria and yeast	✓	□	□
revised twice – all questions right	✓	✓	✓	Specialised cells	✓	□	□
				Diffusion	✓	□	□
Move on to another topic when you have all three ticks				Tissues and organs	✓	✓	□
				Organ systems	✓	□	□

Student Book
pages 16–17 **B2**

2.1 Photosynthesis

Photosynthesis can only be carried out by green plants and algae.

- Chlorophyll in the chloroplasts absorbs the Sun's **light energy.**
- The equation for photosynthesis is:

$$\text{carbon dioxide} + \text{water} \xrightarrow{\text{(+ light energy)}} \text{glucose} + \text{oxygen}$$

The process for photosynthesis is:

1 Carbon dioxide is taken in by the leaves, and water is taken up by the roots.
2 The chlorophyll traps the light energy needed for photosynthesis.
3 This energy is used to convert the carbon dioxide and water into **glucose** (a sugar).

- Oxygen is released as a by-product of photosynthesis.
- Some of the glucose is converted into insoluble starch for storage.
- By testing leaves with iodine solution (the **iodine test** for starch) we can identify the starch in the leaf and show that photosynthesis has occurred. Variegated leaves have patches of green (with chlorophyll) and white (without chlorophyll). Only the green patches will turn the iodine solution blue-black to show that starch has been made.

▷ 1 *Where does the energy for photosynthesis come from?*

Key words: light energy, glucose, variegated

Key points

- During photosynthesis light energy is transferred to chemical energy.
- Leaves are well adapted for photosynthesis.

AQA Examiner's tip

Make sure you know the word equation for photosynthesis – it often comes up in questions.

These variegated leaves came from a plant which has been kept in the light for several hours. The one on the right has been tested for starch, using iodine solution.

Student Book
pages 18–19 **B2**

2.2 Limiting factors

- A lack of light would slow down the rate of photosynthesis as light provides the energy for the process. Even on sunny days, light may be limited to plants which are shaded by trees.
- If it is cold, then enzymes do not work effectively and this will slow down the rate of photosynthesis.
- If there is too little carbon dioxide, then the rate of photosynthesis will slow down. Carbon dioxide may be limited in an enclosed space, e.g. in a greenhouse on a sunny day where there is plenty of light energy available but the plants run out of carbon dioxide.

▷1 *Why do enzyme reactions slow down?*

- Anything which puts a cap on the rate of photosynthesis is a **limiting factor**.

When doing photosynthesis experiments you need to know which factor is being changed and which factors must be controlled. If you want to find out the effect of increasing carbon dioxide levels then you must be aware that other factors such as light may limit the rate of photosynthesis.

- The **independent variable** is the one being tested, e.g. concentration of carbon dioxide.
- The **dependent variable** is the one you measure – in this case it is usually the volume of oxygen produced.

Key points

- Plants grow best when they have enough light, carbon dioxide and water, and are kept at a suitable temperature.
- If any of these conditions are not met, the rate of photosynthesis will be limited.

Bump up your grade

To get the best marks possible, make sure you can explain why a factor is limiting. The most difficult questions involve interpretation of graphs. Always check the axes of the graph to work out which are the independent and dependent variables.

● Variables which need to be controlled are light, temperature and the type of plant being used.

▶ **2** *What is meant by the term 'dependent variable'?*

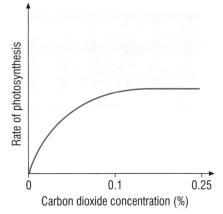

The effect of increasing carbon dioxide levels on the rate of photosynthesis at a particular light level and temperature. Eventually one of the other factors becomes limiting.

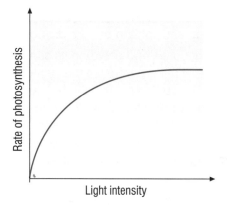

The effect of light intensity on the rate of photosynthesis

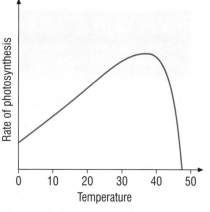

The rate of photosynthesis increases steadily with a rise in temperature up to a certain point. After this the enzymes are destroyed and the reaction stops completely.

Key words: limiting factor, independent variable, dependent variable

---

Student Book
pages 20–21

B2

2.3 How plants use glucose

Key points

● Plant and algal cells produce glucose during photosynthesis.

● Glucose produced in photosynthesis can be used in a variety of ways.

● Plants and algae also need nitrate ions to make proteins.

The uses of soluble glucose

● The glucose produced by photosynthesis may be:
  – converted into insoluble starch for storage
  – used for respiration
  – converted into fats and oils for storage
  – used to produce cellulose which strengthens cell walls
  – used to produce proteins.
● Plant and algal cells also need a supply of **mineral ions** such as **nitrate ions** in order to produce protein. Plants absorb nitrate ions from the soil. Algae absorb nitrate ions from the water they live in.

▶ **1** *Name three substances used for storage in plants.*

Key words: mineral ion, nitrate ion

AQA *Examiner's tip*

Remember that although glucose is a sugar it can be converted into other substances which the plants or algae need.

Student Book
pages 22–23
B2

2.4 Making the most of photosynthesis ⚙️●

Key points

- Temperature, light levels and carbon dioxide levels affect the rate of photosynthesis.
- Plant growers can artificially control the environment to improve plant growth.

By controlling the temperature, light and carbon dioxide levels in a greenhouse like this you can produce the biggest possible crops – fast!

- Plant growers try to give their plants the best conditions for growth by controlling the environment.
- They have to evaluate the benefits of increasing growth with the increased cost of heating and lighting or from providing carbon dioxide.
- Greenhouses and polytunnels can be constructed to grow plants in an enclosed space. If the greenhouse has heaters and lamps the rate of photosynthesis will increase but may stop if the temperature or light intensity is too high. By adding carbon dioxide to the air in the greenhouse the rate of photosynthesis will also increase. Nitrate ions can also be added to the soil to ensure that plants can make the proteins needed for healthy growth.
- It can be expensive to provide a suitable temperature, light and carbon dioxide. The grower has to compare the **biomass** of plants grown indoors and outdoors without these extra factors.

▷ **1** *What factors must be controlled in a greenhouse to improve plant growth?*

Key word: biomass

Student Book
pages 24–25
B2

2.5 Organisms in their environment

Key points

- The distribution of organisms is affected by environmental factors.
- Animals as well as plants are affected by physical factors.

AQA *Examiner's tip*

If you are given data about the distribution of organisms, look for reasons why plants might not be able to grow there. Plants supply food for animals so fewer plants results in fewer animals.

Living organisms form communities. It is important to understand the relationships within and between these communities. These relationships can be influenced by external factors. Physical factors that may affect the distribution of organisms are:

- **Temperature** – for example, arctic plants are small which limits the number of plant eaters which can survive in the area.
- **Availability of nutrients** – most plants struggle to grow when mineral ions are in short supply and again few animals will survive in that area.
- **Amount of light** – few plants live on a forest floor because the light is blocked out by the trees. Shaded plants often have broader leaves or more chlorophyll.
- **Availability of water** – water is important for all organisms so few will live in a desert. If it rains in the desert then plants grow, produce flowers and seeds very quickly. Then there will be food for animals.
- **Availability of oxygen** – water animals can be affected by lack of oxygen. Some invertebrates can live at very low oxygen levels, but most fish need high levels of oxygen dissolved in water.
- **Availability of carbon dioxide** – lack of carbon dioxide will affect plant growth and consequently the food available for animals.

▷ **1** *Why are there so few animals living in very cold regions such as the Arctic?*

Student Book
pages 26–27

B2

2.6 Measuring the distribution of organisms

Key points

- The distribution of living things in their natural environment can be measured.

- The data can be used to find the range, mean, median and mode of the measurements.

AQA Examiner's tip

Remember that quadrats can be placed randomly or along a line transect. Think about which method should be used in different situations.

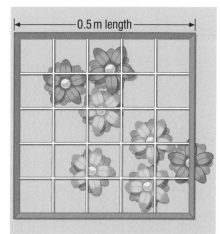

With plants partly covered by the quadrat, decide whether they are in or out *and stick to it.* In this quadrat, you have six or seven plants per 0.25 m² (that's 24 or 28 plants per square metre), depending on the way you count.

Quantitative data can be used to describe how physical factors might be affecting the distribution of organisms in a particular habitat. Quantitative data can be obtained by:

- random **quantitative sampling** using a quadrat

- sampling along a **transect**.

A **quadrat** is a square frame made of metal or wood which may be subdivided into a grid. If several quadrats are placed randomly in a field the investigator can count the number of a particular type of plant or animal in each quadrat. This can be used to estimate the number of, for example, daisies in the whole field.

- **Sample size** is important. In a large field enough random quadrats must be placed to be sure the sample is representative of the whole field.

- An estimate of the number of, for example, daisies is usually given as a mean per square metre.

A transect is not random. A line is marked between two points, e.g. from the top of a rocky shore down to the sea. A quadrat can be placed every five metres along the line and the organisms counted. Physical factors could also be measured at each quadrat point. This method supplies a lot of information about the habitat and the organisms in it.

▶ 1 *What is a quadrat?*

Maths skills

You need to understand the terms **range, mean, median** and **mode** when recording quantitative data.

The following readings are the numbers of daisies counted in eleven 1 m² quadrats:

10   11   <u>20</u>   15   11   10   18   20   10   13   <u>5</u>

The **range** is the difference between the minimum and maximum readings: in this case the range of the daisies is 20 − 5 = 15 per m².

The **mean** is the sum of the readings divided by the number of readings taken: in this case the mean is 143/11 = 13 per m².

The **median** is the middle value of the readings when written in order:

5   10   10   10   11   **11**   13   15   18   20   20

In this case it is the sixth value out of the eleven readings, so the median is 11 per m².

The **mode** is the reading which appears the most frequently: in this case the mode is 10 per m².

Key words: quantitative sampling, transect, quadrat, sample size, range, mean, median, mode

2.7 How valid is the data?

Key points

- The method used in an investigation must answer the question which has been asked.

- Measurements must be repeatable and reproducible.

- All the variables should be controlled in a valid investigation.

Bump up your grade

You will improve your grade if you can use all the mathematical terms involved in data analysis and make sure you understand the difference between repeatability and reproducibility.

- Investigations about distribution of organisms in their environment can be very difficult. That is because they are often done over a long period of time and not all variables can be controlled.

- If a transect is made at a beach during the morning, a comparative investigation must be done at the same time of day even if it is two months later. The time of day is a control variable. We can control this variable. In a **valid** investigation all possible **variables** must be controlled.

- A measurement is **repeatable** if the original experimenter repeats the investigation using the same method and equipment and obtains the same results. However, sometimes the experimenter may be making the same mistake every time and get repeatable results! So it may also be necessary to check the results to ensure they are **reproducible**.

- A measurement is reproducible if the investigation is repeated by another person, or by using different equipment or techniques, and the same results are obtained.

- Sample size is an important factor in order to get valid, repeatable and reproducible results. If the sample is too small it may not be representative. So the larger the sample size, the more trust we can have in the data generated in an environmental investigation.

▶ **1** *How can you make sure an investigation is valid?*

Key words: valid, variable, repeatable, reproducible

1 Name the solution used to test a leaf for starch.

2 What is the result of the iodine test for starch?

3 What is the word equation for photosynthesis?

4 Give three physical factors which affect the distribution of plants.

5 Why would there be little point in heating a greenhouse on a summer's day?

6 What is meant by the term 'limiting factor' in photosynthesis?

7 How can you use a quadrat to make a line transect?

8 What is the difference between a mean and a median?

9 Why is it difficult to be sure an investigation in outdoor habitats is valid?

10 What is meant by 'reproducible' results?

Chapter checklist			
Tick when you have:			
reviewed it after your lesson	✓ ☐ ☐	Photosynthesis	☐ ☐ ☐
revised once – some questions right	✓ ✓ ☐	Limiting factors	☐ ☐ ☐
revised twice – all questions right	✓ ✓ ✓	How plants use glucose	☐ ☐ ☐
Move on to another topic when you have all three ticks		Making the most of photosynthesis	☐ ☐ ☐
		Organisms in their environment	☐ ☐ ☐
		Measuring the distribution of organisms	☐ ☐ ☐
		How valid is the data?	☐ ☐ ☐

Student Book
pages 32–33 **B2**

3.1 Proteins, catalysts and enzymes

Key points

- Proteins are made of long chains of amino acids.
- Proteins have many different functions.
- Enzymes are proteins which act as biological catalysts.

AQA **Examiner's tip**

Enzymes are very important proteins; but don't forget that proteins have other functions too.

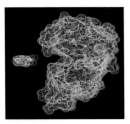

Enzymes are made-up of chains of amino acids folded together, as you can see in this computer-generated image

- Protein molecules are made of long chains of amino acids.
- The long chains are folded to produce specific shapes. The shape of a protein depends on its function.
- Proteins can be:
  - structural components of tissues, such as muscle
  - hormones
  - antibodies
  - **catalysts.**

▐▐▌➡ **1** *What are proteins made of?*

Chemical reactions in cells are controlled by proteins called **enzymes**.

- Enzymes are **biological catalysts** – they speed-up reactions.
- Enzymes are large proteins and the shape of the enzyme is vital for its function. This shape has an area where other molecules can fit – the '**active site**'.
- The **substrate** in a reaction can be held in the active site and either be connected to another molecule or be broken down.
- Enzymes can:
  - build large molecules from many smaller ones, e.g. building starch from glucose molecules
  - change one molecule into another one, e.g. convert one type of sugar into another
  - break down large molecules into smaller ones, e.g. all the digestive enzymes do this.

Key words: catalyst, enzyme, active site, substrate

Student Book
pages 34–35 **B2**

3.2 Factors affecting enzyme action

Key points

- Factors which alter the shape of the active site prevent the enzyme from working.
- Enzyme activity is affected by temperature and pH.

Optimum temperature – this is when the reaction works as fast as possible

The rate of the reaction increases with the increase in temperature

The enzyme is denatured and stops working

Rate of reaction

Temperature (°C)

Enzyme reactions are similar to other reactions when the temperature is increased.

- Reactions take place faster when it is warmer. At higher temperatures the molecules move around more quickly and so collide with each other more often, and with more energy.
- If the temperature gets too hot the enzyme stops working because the active site changes shape. We say that the enzyme becomes **denatured**.
- Each enzyme works best at a particular pH value. Some work best in acid conditions, such as the stomach, but others need neutral or alkaline conditions.
- If the pH is too acidic or alkaline for the enzyme, then the active site could change shape. Then the enzyme becomes denatured.

▐▐▌➡ **1** *What is meant by the term 'denatured'?*

Key word: denatured

The rate of an enzyme-controlled reaction increases as the temperature rises – but only until the point where the complex protein structure of the enzyme breaks down

Student Book
pages 36–37 **B2**

3.3 Enzymes in digestion

Key points

- Digestive enzymes are made by glands in the digestive system.
- Digestive enzymes work outside the body cells in the cavity of the digestive system.
- Specific enzymes digest each particular food type.

AQA *Examiner's tip*

Memorise the three main digestive enzymes. Learn their substrates and the products of digestion.

Some enzymes work outside the body cells. Digestive enzymes are produced by specialised cells in glands and in the lining of the gut. The enzymes pass out of the cells and come into contact with the food. **Digestion** involves the breakdown of large, insoluble molecules into smaller soluble molecules.

Each reaction is controlled by a specific enzyme.

- **Amylase** (a **carbohydrase**) is produced by the salivary glands, the pancreas and the small intestine. Amylase catalyses the digestion of starch into sugars in the mouth and small intestine.
- **Protease** is produced by the stomach, the pancreas and the small intestine. Protease catalyses the breakdown of proteins into amino acids in the stomach and small intestine.
- **Lipase** is produced by the pancreas and small intestine. Lipase catalyses the breakdown of **lipids** (fats and oils) to **fatty acids** and **glycerol**.

▶ **1** *Which enzyme digests starch?*

Key words: digestion, amylase, carbohydrase, protease, lipase, lipid, fatty acid, glycerol

Student Book
pages 38–39 **B2**

3.4 Speeding up digestion

Key points

- Enzymes work best in a narrow pH range.

AQA *Examiner's tip*

Remember that bile is produced in the liver and stored in the gall bladder. Bile only neutralises acid, it does not contain enzymes.

- Protease enzymes in the stomach work best in acid conditions. Glands in the stomach wall produce hydrochloric acid to create very acidic conditions.
- Amylase and lipase work in the small intestine. They work best when the conditions are slightly alkaline.
- The liver produces **bile** that is stored in the gall bladder. The alkaline bile is squirted into the small intestine and neutralises the stomach acid. Bile makes the conditions in the small intestine slightly alkaline.

▶ **1** *Where is bile produced?*

Key word: bile

Student Book
pages 40–41

B2

3.5 Making use of enzymes

Key points

- Microorganisms produce enzymes that we can use.
- Enzymes can be used in products in the home and in industry.

Learning to eat solid food isn't easy. Having some of it pre-digested by protease enzymes can make it easier to get the nutrients you need to grow.

Some microorganisms produce enzymes that pass out of their cells. These enzymes have many uses in industry but can be costly to produce.

- **Biological detergents** contain proteases and lipases that digest food stains. They work at lower temperatures than ordinary washing powders. This saves energy and money spent on electricity.
- Proteases are used to pre-digest proteins in some baby foods.
- **Isomerase** is used to convert glucose syrup into **fructose syrup**. Fructose is much sweeter, so less is needed in foods. The foods, therefore, are not so fattening.
- Carbohydrases are used to convert starch into sugar syrup for use in foods.
- In industry, enzymes are used to bring about reactions at normal temperatures and pressures. Traditional chemical processes require expensive equipment and a lot of energy to produce high temperatures and pressures.

▐▐▐▶ **1 Which enzyme is used to convert glucose into fructose?**

AQA *Examiner's tip*

Make sure you understand the advantages of using enzymes in industry.

Key words: biological detergent, isomerase, fructose syrup

Student Book
pages 42–43

B2

3.6 High-tech enzymes

Key points

- There are advantages and disadvantages to using enzymes in industry and the home.

Bump up your grade

To improve your grade make sure you understand how enzymes work and what factors affect them. Practise reading graphs relating to enzyme investigations. Nearly every exam has an enzyme question!

Advantages of using enzymes:

- Enzymes in biological washing powders are very effective at removing stains such as blood, grass and gravy.
- Biological washing powders can be used at lower temperatures. This saves energy and reduces costs.
- Some enzymes are used in medicine to diagnose, control or even cure disease.
- In industry, costs of equipment and energy can be reduced.

Possible disadvantages of using enzymes:

- If people misuse washing powders they may have allergic reactions on their skin. The enzymes are enclosed in capsules in the dry powder. Once the powder is dissolved, hands should not be placed in the water.
- Enzymes may enter waterways via the sewage system.
- Industrial enzymes can be costly to produce.
- Enzymes denature at the high temperatures needed to kill pathogens in the washing.
- Some fabrics such as wool will be digested by proteases.

▐▐▐▶ **1 How do enzymes get into rivers?**

1 Which two factors can alter the shape of an enzyme?

2 Where is amylase produced?

3 What are the products of lipid (fat) digestion?

4 Which acid is produced by the stomach?

5 What is the function of bile?

6 Why are proteases used in baby foods?

7 Give two types of reaction controlled by enzymes in the cells.

8 Why does increasing the temperature increase the rate of a reaction?

9 Give one advantage and one disadvantage of using enzymes in industry.

10 Why do biological washing powders work more efficiently than non-biological powders?

Chapter checklist	✓ ✓ ✓
Tick when you have:	Proteins, catalysts and enzymes ☐ ☐ ☐
reviewed it after your lesson ✓ ☐ ☐	Factors affecting enzyme action ☐ ☐ ☐
revised once – some questions right ✓ ✓ ☐	Enzymes in digestion ☐ ☐ ☐
revised twice – all questions right ✓ ✓ ✓	Speeding up digestion ☐ ☐ ☐
Move on to another topic when you have all three ticks	Making use of enzymes ☐ ☐ ☐
	High-tech enzymes ☐ ☐ ☐

Student Book
pages 46–47

B2

4.1 Aerobic respiration

Aerobic respiration takes place continually in plants and animals. The process uses glucose and oxygen to release energy. Carbon dioxide and water are produced as waste products. Most of the chemical reactions of aerobic respiration take place in the mitochondria and are controlled by enzymes.

- The equation for aerobic respiration is:

glucose + oxygen → carbon dioxide + water [**+energy**]

The energy released may be used by the organism to:

- Build larger molecules from smaller ones.
- Enable muscle contraction in animals.
- Maintain a constant body temperature in colder surroundings in mammals and birds.
- Build sugars, nitrates and other nutrients into amino acids and then proteins in plants.

IIIII➡ 1 *Where does aerobic respiration take place?*

Investigations involving aerobic respiration usually measure the volume of carbon dioxide produced. Limewater is used to detect carbon dioxide. The limewater turns cloudy. The quicker the limewater turns cloudy the faster carbon dioxide is being produced. It is also possible to detect a rise in temperature when respiration is occurring. If germinating peas are left in a thermos flask, the rise in temperature due to respiration can be monitored.

Key points

- Aerobic respiration is the release of energy from food when oxygen is available.
- Most of the reactions for aerobic respiration take place in the mitochondria.

AQA Examiner's tip

Remember that plants as well as animals respire. During daylight the plants use the carbon dioxide released in respiration for photosynthesis.

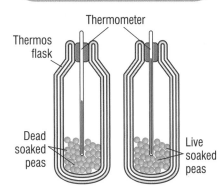

When peas respire they release energy which heats the surroundings

Student Book
pages 48–49

B2

4.2 The effect of exercise on the body

- When you exercise, your muscles need more energy so that they can contract.
- You need to increase the rate at which oxygen and glucose reach the muscle cells for aerobic respiration. You also need to remove the extra waste carbon dioxide produced more quickly.
- The heart rate increases and the blood vessels supplying the muscles dilate (widen). This allows more blood containing oxygen and glucose to reach the muscles.
- Your breathing rate and the depth of each breath also increase. This allows a greater uptake of oxygen and release of carbon dioxide at the lungs.
- Muscles store glucose as **glycogen**. The glycogen can be converted back to glucose for use during exercise.

IIIII➡ 1 *Which sugar is needed by the muscles for aerobic respiration?*

Key points

- During exercise muscles need more energy.
- More glucose and oxygen need to be transported to the muscles.
- To do this there are changes in heart rate, in breathing and in blood supply to the actively respiring muscle cells.

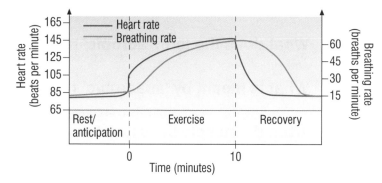

During exercise, the heart rate and breathing rate increase to supply the muscles with glucose and oxygen and to remove the extra carbon dioxide produced

Key word: glycogen

Student Book
pages 50–51

B2

4.3 Anaerobic respiration

Key points

- When muscles work hard for a long time they may have too little oxygen and become fatigued.
- Muscles use anaerobic respiration if they are short of oxygen.
- When muscles respire anaerobically they build up an oxygen debt. **[H]**

Repeated movements can soon lead to anaerobic respiration in your muscles – particularly if you're not used to it

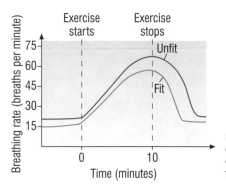

Hard exercise means everyone has to pay off their oxygen debt – but if you are fit you can pay it off faster!

- If you use muscles over a long period then they will get tired (fatigued) and stop contracting efficiently. For example, this might happen when you lift a weight repeatedly for a few minutes or go jogging.
- When your muscles cannot get enough oxygen for aerobic respiration, they start to respire anaerobically.
- The glucose is not completely broken down in anaerobic respiration and **lactic acid** is produced.
- Less energy is released from the glucose in anaerobic respiration.
- One cause of muscle fatigue is the build up of lactic acid.
- Blood flowing through the muscles removes the lactic acid.

What is produced during anaerobic respiration?

Anaerobic respiration is inefficient because the breakdown of glucose is not complete. Instead of carbon dioxide and water, lactic acid is produced as a waste product.

Lactic acid causes muscle fatigue. When the exercise has finished this lactic acid must be completely broken down. You still need to take in a lot of oxygen to do this. The extra oxygen needed is known as the 'oxygen debt'. Eventually the oxygen oxidises lactic acid into carbon dioxide and water.

AQA *Examiner's tip*

Remember that it is the lactic acid that causes fatigue (tiredness).

When you stop your exercise you must get rid of this lactic acid build-up. You keep breathing in a lot of oxygen to do this. Warming down after exercise helps to break down the lactic acid.

Key words: lactic acid, oxygen debt

Higher

1 What does the term 'aerobic' mean?

2 What is meant by 'anaerobic' respiration?

3 What do muscle cells need more of during exercise?

4 What are the two waste products of aerobic respiration?

5 Which substance is stored in the muscles and can be converted into glucose?

6 What is the word equation for aerobic respiration?

7 Why do muscles become fatigued (tired) during vigorous exercise?

8 What changes occur to the breathing and heart rate during exercise?

9 Why do blood vessels in the muscles dilate during exercise?

10 Explain what is meant by an 'oxygen debt'. [H]

Chapter checklist	✓	✓	✓
Tick when you have:	Aerobic respiration	☐ ☐ ☐
reviewed it after your lesson ✓ ☐ ☐	The effect of exercise on the body	☐ ☐ ☐
revised once – some questions right ✓ ✓ ☐		
revised twice – all questions right ✓ ✓ ✓	Anaerobic respiration	☐ ☐ ☐
Move on to another topic when you have all three ticks		

Student Book
pages 54–55

B2

5.1 Cell division and growth

- In body cells, chromosomes are found in pairs.

- Body cells need to divide to produce new cells for growth or repair.

- Mitosis is the type of cell division that produces identical new cells.

- Animal cells differentiate early in development but many plant cells maintain the ability to differentiate throughout their life.

AQA *Examiner's tip*

Learn the word 'mitosis' – two identical cells are made.

Mitosis = making identical two

- Cell division is necessary for the growth of an organism, or for the repair of damaged tissues.

- **Mitosis** results in two identical cells being produced from the original cell.

- The chromosomes contain the genes (**alleles**) which must be passed on to each new cell.

- A copy of each chromosome is made before the cell divides and one of each chromosome goes to each new cell.

- In early development of animal and plant embryos the cells are unspecialised and are called **stem cells**.

- Most animal cells differentiate early in development and cell division is mainly for repair and replacement.

- Plants cells can differentiate throughout the life of the plant as it continues to grow.

- Cells of offspring produced by asexual reproduction are produced by mitosis from the parent cell. They contain the same alleles as the parents.

> **1** *Which type of cell division produces two identical cells from the original cell?*

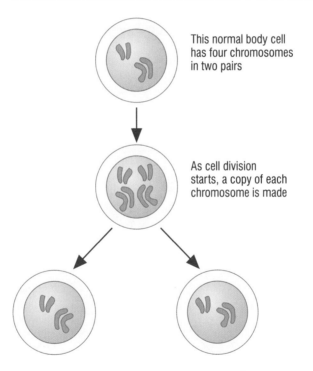

This normal body cell has four chromosomes in two pairs

As cell division starts, a copy of each chromosome is made

The cell divides in two to form two daughter cells. Each daughter cell has a nucleus containing four chromosomes identical to the ones in the original parent cell.

Two identical cells are formed by the simple division that takes place during mitosis. For simplicity this cell is shown with only two pairs of chromosomes (there are actually 23 pairs).

Key words: mitosis, allele, stem cell

5.2 Cell division in sexual reproduction

● Cells in reproductive organs, e.g. testes and ovaries, divide by **meiosis** to form sex cells (gametes). In humans the gametes are the sperm and **ova**.

● Each gamete has only one chromosome from each original pair. All of the cells are different from each other and the parent cell.

● Sexual reproduction results in variation as the gametes from each parent fuse. So half the genetic information comes from the father and half from the mother.

● When gametes join at fertilisation, a single body cell with new pairs of chromosomes is formed.

● A new individual then develops by this cell repeatedly dividing by mitosis.

▐▐▐▶ **1** *What type of cells are produced by meiosis?*

Key points

● Gametes (sex cells) are produced by meiosis.

● Gametes have one set of chromosomes; body cells have two sets.

● Sexual reproduction gives rise to variation.

AQA *Examiner's tip*

Don't confuse the two types of cell division.

Eggs and sperm are made by meiosis. **Me**iosis = **m**aking **e**ggs

Meiosis

● Before division, a copy of each chromosome is made.

● The cell now divides twice to form four gametes (sex cells).

● Each gamete has a single set of chromosomes each with a different combination of genes.

▐▐▐▶ **2** *Explain how four gametes are formed from one cell.*

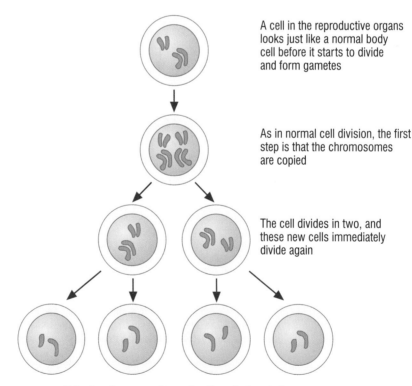

A cell in the reproductive organs looks just like a normal body cell before it starts to divide and form gametes

As in normal cell division, the first step is that the chromosomes are copied

The cell divides in two, and these new cells immediately divide again

This gives four sex cells, each with a single set of chromosomes – in this case two instead of the original four

The formation of sex cells in the ovaries and testes involves meiosis to halve the chromosome number. The original cell is shown with only two pairs of chromosomes to make it easier to follow what is happening. [H]

Key words: meiosis, ova

Student Book
pages 58–59

B2

5.3 Stem cells

- Stem cells are not specialised, but can differentiate into many different types of cell when required.
- Stem cells can be used to cure some disorders.

AQA *Examiner's tip*

Remember that stem cells are not specialised. They can change into particular body cells – they differentiate.

- Stem cells are unspecialised.
- Stem cells are found in the human embryo and in adult bone marrow.
- Stem cells change into all the different types of body cell, e.g. nerve cells, muscle cells. We say the cells differentiate.
- Layers of cells in the embryo differentiate into all the cells the body needs.
- Stem cells in the adult bone marrow can change into other types of cell, e.g. blood cells.
- It is hoped that human stem cells can be made to differentiate into many types of cell. The cells formed could then be used to treat conditions such as paralysis, e.g. by differentiating into new nerve cells.

1 *Where are stem cells found in adult humans?*

Student Book
pages 60–61

B2

5.4 From Mendel to DNA

- Gregor Mendel worked out how characteristics are inherited.
- Genes make up the chromosomes, which control our characteristics.
- Chromosomes are large molecules of DNA.
- A gene is a small section of DNA.
- Everyone (except identical twins) has unique DNA.

- Gregor Mendel was a monk who worked out how characteristics were inherited. Mendel was the first person to suggest the idea of separately inherited 'factors'.
- It took a long time for Mendel's ideas to be accepted. That was because scientists did not know about chromosomes and genes until after Mendel died.
- Mendel's 'factors' are now called genes. Genes are found on chromosomes.
- Chromosomes are made of DNA which is a very long molecule with a double helix structure.
- Genes are short sections of DNA.
- Every individual, except for identical twins, has different DNA. This unique DNA pattern can be used to identify people by their **DNA fingerprint.**

1 *Which scientist worked out how characteristics are inherited?*

Genetic code
Each gene codes for a particular combination (order) of amino acids which make a specific protein.

2 *What does a gene code for?*

Key word: DNA fingerprint

Higher

5.5 Inheritance in action

- Human beings have 23 pairs of chromosomes, one pair are the **sex chromosomes**. Human females have two X chromosomes (XX) and males have an X and a Y chromosome (XY).
- Genes controlling the same characteristic are called alleles.
- If an allele 'masks' the effect of another it is said to be '**dominant**'. The allele where the effect is 'masked' is said to be '**recessive**'.
- Genetic diagrams, including family trees, illustrate how alleles and characteristics are inherited.

▐▐▐▶ **1** *Which sex chromosomes are found in human males?*

Genetic terms and models

Genetic diagrams are biological models which can be constructed to predict and explain the inheritance of particular characteristics. Punnet squares are grids used to insert the alleles' symbols.

It is important to use the correct terminology.

Phenotype – **ph**ysical appearance of the characteristic, e.g. dimples or no dimples.

Genotype – the **g**enetic make up – which alleles does the individual inherit? DD, Dd or dd.

Homozygous – both alleles are the same DD (homozygous dominant) or dd (homozygous recessive).

Heterozygous – the two alleles are different Dd.

▐▐▐▶ **2** *What is meant by the term 'phenotype'?*

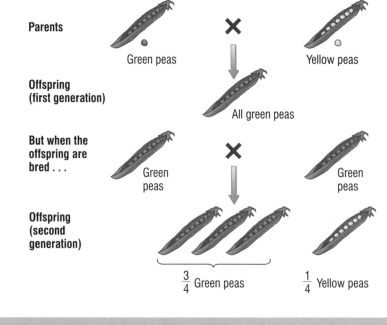

Key words: sex chromosome, dominant, recessive

5.6 Inherited conditions in humans

Key points

- Some disorders are caused by genes and can be inherited.
- Polydactyly is caused by a dominant allele.
- Cystic fibrosis is caused by a recessive allele.
- Genetic diagrams are used to predict the chances of inheriting the disorder.

AQA **Examiner's tip**

Remember there are only three combinations of alleles:

AA Aa aa

Look at family trees to decide which combination each person has.

Don't be put off by the different symbols used in a question.

Use the symbols given in the question to construct a Punnet square. **[H]**

- There are many different **genetic disorders**. Some are caused by a dominant allele, some by a recessive allele.
- If the allele is dominant the person only has to inherit one dominant allele to have the genetic disorder, e.g. **polydactyly** where a baby is born with extra fingers or toes.
- Polydactyly can be passed on by one parent who has the allele.
- If an allele is recessive the person must inherit two recessive alleles to have the disorder.
- **Cystic fibrosis** is caused by a recessive allele. The allele affects cell membranes and causes the production of thick sticky mucus. The mucus can affect several organs, including the lungs and pancreas.
- A child must inherit a recessive allele from both parents to develop cystic fibrosis. The disorder can be passed on from two parents who don't have cystic fibrosis themselves. The parents are described as **carriers** of the allele.
- By using genetic diagrams it is possible to see how a disorder (or allele) has been inherited and to predict whether future offspring will inherit it.

▐▐▌➡ **1** *Name a genetic disorder which is controlled by a dominant allele.*

Genetic disorders

If a parent is heterozygous for polydactyly each child has a 50% chance of inheriting the disorder.

If both parents are heterozygous for cystic fibrosis each child has a 25% chance of inheriting the disorder.

The outcomes of genetic crosses can be shown on a Punnet square.

▐▐▌➡ **2** *What are the chances of a child having cystic fibrosis if one parent has the disorder and the other parent is heterozygous?*

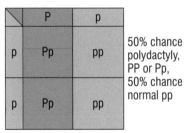

50% chance polydactyly, PP or Pp, 50% chance normal pp

Pp = Parent with polydactyly
pp = Normal parent

A genetic diagram (Punnet square) for polydactyly

Both parents are carriers, so Cc

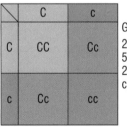

Genotype:
25% normal (CC)
50% carriers (Cc)
25% affected by cystic fibrosis (cc)

Phenotype:
3/4, or 75% chance normal
1/4, or 25% chance cystic fibrosis

A genetic diagram (Punnet square) for cystic fibrosis

Key words: genetic disorder, polydactyly, cystic fibrosis, carrier

Key points

- Embryonic stem cells can be used in medical research and treatments.
- Embryos can be screened for genetic disorders.
- There are economic, social and ethical issues concerning the use of embryos and in embryo screening.

Bump up your grade

To improve your grade, always look at both sides of an argument about the use of embryos and try to write a balanced account. Your conclusion should be based on the argument you have given.

5.7 Stem cells and embryos – science and ethics

- Adult stem cells, e.g. bone marrow cells, are useful in treating some disorders such as leukaemia.
- More recently, doctors have investigated the use of embryonic stem cells which have the potential to differentiate into a wide variety of cells.
- Embryonic stem cells are taken from spare embryos from IVF **or** created from adult cells **or** may be taken from the umbilical cord of newborn babies.
- Embryonic stem cells could be used to grow new tissues and organs for transplant.
- Some people are concerned about the use of embryos because the research is experimental, the embryos have the potential to be babies and are destroyed, the embryo cannot give permission, and the research is expensive.
- Embryo screening involves tests to diagnose disorders before the baby is born.
- The results of the test may give the parents choices. Sometimes the parents decide to terminate the pregnancy. Other parents decide this is not ethical but can prepare for the delivery of an affected baby.
- In IVF the embryos are screened and only healthy embryos are implanted into the mother. Embryos carrying faulty genes are destroyed and some people think this is unethical.

▮▮▮➤ **1** *What is embryo screening?*

1 Why do cells divide by mitosis?

2 How many chromosomes does a human have in each body cell?

3 Which type of cell division produces sex cells?

4 What molecule are genes made of?

5 What are 'alleles'?

6 Why does sexual reproduction result in variation?

7 Explain why offspring produced by asexual reproduction are genetically identical.

8 What is meant by the term 'genotype'? [H]

9 What do we mean by a 'heterozygous' individual? [H]

10 What are the chances of a child having polydactyly if one parent is heterozygous and the other parent is homozygous recessive? [H]

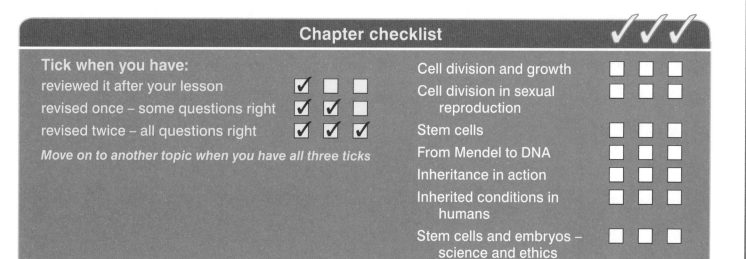

Chapter checklist	✓	✓	✓
Tick when you have:			
reviewed it after your lesson [✓][ ][ ]	Cell division and growth	☐	☐	☐
revised once – some questions right [✓][✓][ ]	Cell division in sexual reproduction	☐	☐	☐
revised twice – all questions right [✓][✓][✓]	Stem cells	☐	☐	☐
Move on to another topic when you have all three ticks	From Mendel to DNA	☐	☐	☐
	Inheritance in action	☐	☐	☐
	Inherited conditions in humans	☐	☐	☐
	Stem cells and embryos – science and ethics	☐	☐	☐

6.1 The origins of life on Earth

Key points

- Scientists cannot be exact about when life began on Earth because there is little repeatable or reproducible evidence.

- Fossils are the remains of organisms from many years ago which are found in rocks.

- We can learn from fossils how different organisms have changed as life developed on Earth.

This amazing fossil shows two dinosaurs – prehistoric animals which died out millions of years before we appeared on Earth. Fossils can only give us a brief glimpse into the past. We will never know exactly what disaster snuffed out the life of these spectacular reptiles all those years ago.

- It is believed that the Earth is about 4500 million years old and that life began about 3500 million years ago.

- There is some debate as to whether the first life developed due to the conditions on Earth, or whether simple life forms arrived from another planet.

- We can date rocks. Fossils are found in rocks, so we can date when different organisms existed.

- Fossils may be formed in various ways:
  - from the hard parts of animals that do not decay easily, e.g. bones, teeth, shells, claws
  - from parts of organisms that have not decayed because some of the conditions for decay are absent, e.g. fossils of animals preserved in ice
  - when parts of the organism are replaced by other materials, such as minerals, as they decay
  - as preserved traces of organisms, e.g. footprints, burrows and rootlet traces.

- Most organisms that died did not leave a fossil because the exact conditions for fossil formation were not present.

▮▮▮➡ **1** *Name a hard part of an animal which will not decay easily.*

- Many early life forms had soft bodies so few traces were left behind.

- Traces which were left are likely to have been destroyed by geological activity such as earthquakes.

▮▮▮➡ **2** *Why are some fossils destroyed over time?*

Maths skills

The time scales involved in the development of life on Earth are huge.
- 4500 million years is the same as 4.5 billion years or 4 500 000 000
- To save writing a whole string of zeros, it is easier to write 4.5×10^9.
- Try to remember a thousand is 10^3, a million is 10^6 and a billion is 10^9.

AQA Examiner's tip

Remember that soft-bodied organisms did not leave fossils, many organisms did not form fossils and some fossils were destroyed over time. This means that the fossil record is incomplete.

Student Book
pages 72–73 **B2**

6.2 Exploring the fossil evidence

Key points

- The fossil record can show us how much, or how little, organisms have changed over time.
- Many species have evolved and then become extinct.
- Several factors can cause extinction of a species.

Bump up your grade

To improve your grade, always make sure that you mention a change when referring to extinction of a species. If things stay the same, the species will continue to live successfully in its habitat.

- The fossil record is incomplete, but we can learn a lot from fossils which exist. Some organisms have changed a lot over time. Others have changed very little, while some have become extinct.
- **Extinction** means that a species which once existed has completely died out.

Extinction can be caused by a number of factors, but always involves a change in circumstances:

- A new disease may kill all members of a species.
- The environment changes over geological time.
- New diseases may be introduced.
- A new **predator** may evolve or be introduced to an area that effectively kills and eats all of a species.
- A new competitor may evolve or be introduced into an area. The original species may be left with too little to eat.
- A single catastrophic event may occur which destroys the habitat, e.g. a massive volcanic eruption.
- Natural changes in species occur over time.

⟫ **1** *How can a new predator cause extinction of a species?*

Key words: extinction, predator

Student Book
pages 74–75 **B2**

6.3 More about extinction

Key points

- Environmental changes over geological time can cause extinction of organisms.
- A single catastrophic event can also cause extinctions.

AQA Examiner's tip

Remember that no-one knows exactly why the dinosaurs became extinct. There were no scientists around at the time! Ideas suggested are based on the evidence we have. If new evidence is found, such as clues from newly discovered fossils, the ideas could change.

- The biggest influences on species survival are changes in the environment.
- Climate change is an important influence in determining which species survive. A species which is very well adapted to a hot climate may become extinct in an Ice Age. It could be that there is insufficient food or it is too cold to breed.
- Climate change may make it too cold or hot, or wet or dry, for a species and reduce its food supply.
- Fossil evidence shows that there have been mass extinctions on a global scale. Many of the species died out over a period of several million years – a short time in geological terms.
  - The habitat the species lives in may be destroyed by catastrophic events such as a major volcanic eruption.
  - The environment can change dramatically following a collision between a giant asteroid and Earth.
- Why the dinosaurs became extinct has puzzled many scientists. Different ideas have been suggested.
  - The collision of a giant asteroid caused huge fires, earthquakes, landslides and tsunamis. The dust which rose masked the Sun causing darkness and lower temperatures. Plants could not grow and temperatures fell.
  - The extinction was a slower process due to sea ice melting and cooling the sea temperature by about 9 °C, therefore there was less plankton – less food available.

⟫ **1** *Suggest another factor which could have caused the dinosaurs to die out.*

6.4 Isolation and the evolution of new species

Key points

- Natural cycles linked to environmental change result in new species forming and old species dying out.

- New species arise when two populations become isolated.

- In an isolated population alleles are selected that increase the chances of survival in the new environment. **[H]**

- Speciation occurs when the populations become so different that they cannot interbreed. **[H]**

Bump up your grade

To bump up your grade make sure you understand the process of speciation. Write logically using the correct terms.

isolation → genetic variation → alleles selected → interbreeding no longer possible → new species (speciation) **[H]**

- New species can arise from existing species if a group becomes isolated from the rest.

- **Geographical isolation** could occur if an island separates from the mainland or if a new river separates two areas. Mountain ranges and old craters can isolate organisms.

- The organisms left on the island may be exposed to different environmental conditions, food availability or predators. Natural selection will occur in both areas, but different characteristics will be beneficial in the two populations. If the populations are brought together and cannot interbreed, we say that they belong to two separate species.

1 *How do populations become isolated?*

Speciation

- New species can occur following separation of two populations, as in geographical isolation.

- Each population has a wide range of alleles that control their characteristics. This is genetic variation.

- Natural selection will occur in each population. The alleles that control the characteristics which help the organism to survive are selected. The organisms with these alleles will survive and breed.

- If the environment, competitors, food supply and predators are different for each population they will evolve differently.

- **Speciation** has occurred when the two populations can no longer successfully interbreed.

2 *What is meant by genetic variation?*

Darwin's finches

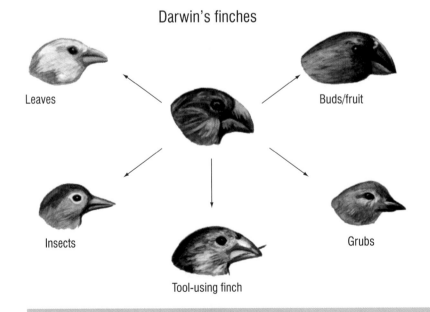

Leaves

Buds/fruit

Insects

Tool-using finch

Grubs

Darwin's finches became isolated on different islands. The conditions, particularly the type of food present, varied on each island. The finches developed differently due to the alleles which were selected in natural selection.

Key words: geographical isolation, speciation

1 How old is the Earth?

2 When do we think life on Earth began?

3 How are fossils dated?

4 Why are there no fossils of early life forms?

5 What is the shortest way to represent three billion in numbers?

6 How might a new competitor cause the extinction of a species?

7 Suggest two ways that people can cause the extinction of some species.

8 What are the two main ideas put forward for the extinction of dinosaurs?

9 What is meant by 'geographical isolation'?

10 What are the stages in speciation?

[H]

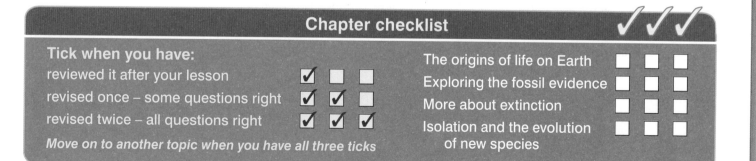

Chapter checklist

Tick when you have:

reviewed it after your lesson ☑ ☐ ☐

revised once – some questions right ☑ ☑ ☐

revised twice – all questions right ☑ ☑ ☑

Move on to another topic when you have all three ticks

The origins of life on Earth ☐ ☐ ☐

Exploring the fossil evidence ☐ ☐ ☐

More about extinction ☐ ☐ ☐

Isolation and the evolution ☐ ☐ ☐
of new species

1 Biological washing powders contain enzymes:

   a   Why are enzymes called biological catalysts?   *(2 marks)*

   b   Most powders contain lipases and proteases. Name the types of foods these enzymes digest and give the products.

       i   Lipases   *(3 marks)*

       ii   Proteases   *(2 marks)*

   c   Non-biological powders can be used to wash clothes at high temperatures. Manufacturers suggest biological powders should be used between 30°C and 40°C. Explain why.   *(2 marks)*

2 Stem cells can be obtained from bone marrow or from embryos.

Bone marrow contains stem cells which produce blood cells. Bone marrow transplants have been used for many years to treat leukaemia, a blood cancer. Most people do not have any concerns about using stem cells from bone marrow.

Embryos can also provide stem cells. It is hoped that many disorders such as paralysis could be treated by using embryo stem cells. Many people think that it is unethical to use embryos in this way.

Use the information and your own knowledge to answer the questions.

   a   What are stem cells?   *(2 marks)*

   b   Why might embryos be a better source of stem cells than bone marrow?   *(2 marks)*

   c   How could embryo stem cells be used to treat paralysis?   *(1 mark)*

   d   Give **one** ethical reason why people object to the use of embryos as a source of stem cells.   *(1 mark)*

3 Many organisms have become extinct while others have evolved into new forms.

   a   Dinosaurs became extinct millions of years ago. How do we know dinosaurs existed?   *(1 mark)*

   b   Many scientists think that the dinosaurs became extinct in a mass extinction when a giant asteroid collided with Earth. A dust cloud rose as a result of the collision. Explain why this event might have caused the extinction of the dinosaurs.   *(3 marks)*

   c   Mass extinctions are relatively rare. Give **two** reasons why a single species may become extinct.   *(2 marks)*

   d   *In this question you will be assessed on using good English, organising information clearly and using specialist terms where appropriate.*

       Describe how a new species may develop as a result of geographic isolation.   **[H]**   *(6 marks)*

4 The diagram below is a genetic diagram that shows a cross between a plant which produces red flowers and one of the same species which produces white flowers.

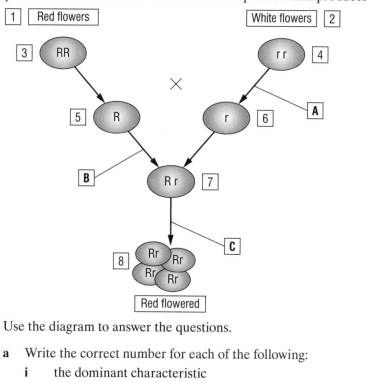

Use the diagram to answer the questions.

a   Write the correct number for each of the following:
   i   the dominant characteristic   (*1 mark*)
   ii   a gamete with a recessive allele   (*1 mark*)
   iii   an embryo   (*1 mark*)

b   Write the correct letter to identify the process:
   i   mitosis   (*1 mark*)
   ii   meiosis   (*1 mark*)
   iii   fertilisation   (*1 mark*)

c   Select the correct word from the list below to copy and complete the sentence:
   alleles   chromosomes   genes
   The letters R and r are symbols to represent ....   (*1 mark*)

d   The diagram below shows another process.

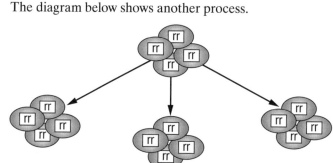

   Use the correct words from the lists to copy and complete the sentences:
   i   The process shown in the second diagram is: ....
         asexual reproduction   fertilisation   sexual reproduction   (*1 mark*)
   ii   The flowers produced by these plants will be: ....
         red   pink   white   (*1 mark*)

Student Book
pages 82–83 **C2**

1.1 Chemical bonding

Key points

- Elements react to form compounds by gaining or losing electrons, or by sharing electrons.

- Atoms of metals in Group 1 combine with atoms of non-metals in Group 7 by transferring electrons to form ions that have the electronic structures of noble gases.

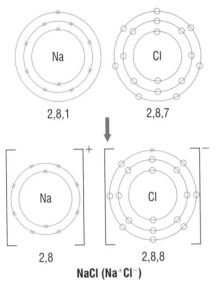

2,8,1   2,8,7

2,8   2,8,8

NaCl (Na⁺Cl⁻)

The formation of sodium chloride (NaCl) is an example of ion formation by transferring an electron

- When two or more elements react together compounds are formed. The atoms of elements join together by sharing electrons or by transferring electrons to achieve stable electronic structures. Atoms of the noble gases have stable electronic structures.

- When atoms of non-metallic elements join together by sharing electrons it is called **covalent bonding**.

> **1** *How can you tell that the compound H_2O has covalent bonds?*

- When metallic elements react with non-metallic elements they produce ionic compounds. The metal atoms lose electrons to form positive **ions**. The atoms of non-metals gain electrons to form negative ions. The ions have the stable electronic structure of a noble gas. The oppositely charged ions attract each other in the ionic compound and this is called **ionic bonding**.

> **2** *Which of these compounds have ionic bonding?*
> *KBr, HCl, H_2S, Na_2O, Cl_2O, MgO*

- Elements in Group 1 of the periodic table have atoms with one electron in their highest occupied energy level (outer shell). Sodium atoms, Na, (electronic structure 2,8,1), form sodium ions, Na^+ (electronic structure 2,8).

- Elements in Group 7 of the periodic table have atoms with seven electrons in their highest occupied energy level (outer shell). Chlorine atoms, Cl (2,8,7) form chloride ions, Cl^- (2,8,8).

- The compound sodium chloride has equal numbers of sodium ions and chloride ions and so we write its formula as NaCl.

> **3** *Explain what happens to the atoms of the elements when lithium reacts with fluorine.*

Key words: covalent bonding, ion, ionic bonding

Student Book
pages 84–85 **C2**

1.2 Ionic bonding

Key points

- Ionic compounds are held together by strong forces between the oppositely charged ions. This is called ionic bonding.

- The ions form a giant structure or lattice. The strong forces of attraction act throughout the lattice.

- We can represent atoms and ions using dot and cross diagrams.

- Ionic bonding holds oppositely charged ions together in **giant structures**. The giant structure of ionic compounds is very regular because the ions all pack together neatly, like marbles in a box.

- Strong electrostatic forces of attraction act in all directions. Each ion in the giant structure or lattice is surrounded by ions with the opposite charge and so is held firmly in place.

- Sodium chloride contains equal numbers of sodium ions and chloride ions as shown by its formula NaCl. The sodium ions and chloride ions alternate to form a cubic lattice.

- The ratio of ions in the structure of an ionic compound depends on the charges on the ions. For example, calcium ions are Ca^{2+} and chloride ions are Cl^-, so calcium chloride contains twice as many chloride ions as calcium ions and its formula is $CaCl_2$.

AQA Examiner's tip

All ionic compounds have giant structures, but you do not need to know the shapes of any structures other than sodium chloride.

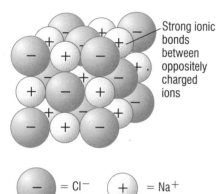

⬤ **= Cl⁻** ⊕ **= Na⁺**

Part of the giant ionic lattice (3D-network) of sodium and chloride ions in sodium chloride

▷ **1** *Why is the formula of sodium chloride NaCl but magnesium chloride is MgCl₂?*

● We can use **dot and cross diagrams** to represent the atoms and ions involved in forming ionic bonds. In these diagrams we only show the electrons in the outermost shell of each atom or ion.

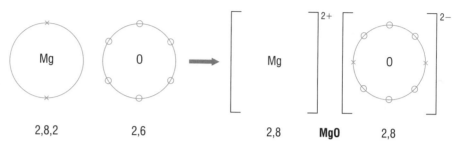

| 2,8,2 | 2,6 | | 2,8 | **MgO** | 2,8 |

When magnesium oxide (MgO) is formed, the reacting magnesium atoms lose two electrons and the oxygen atoms gain two electrons

▷ **2** *Draw a dot and cross diagram to show sodium atoms and chlorine atoms form ions.*

Key words: giant structure or lattice, dot and cross diagram

Student Book
pages 86–87

C2

1.3 Formulae of ionic compounds

Key points

● The charges on the ions in an ionic compound always cancel each other out.

● The formula of an ionic compound shows the ratio of ions present in the compound.

● Sometimes we need brackets to show the ratio of ions in a compound, e.g. magnesium hydroxide, Mg(OH)₂.

● Ionic compounds are neutral. If we know the charge on each ion in a compound we can work out its formula by balancing the charges. Sodium chloride is NaCl (one Na⁺ ion for every one Cl⁻ ion), but calcium chloride is CaCl₂ (one Ca²⁺ ion for every two Cl⁻ ions).

● The charge on simple ions formed by elements in the main groups of the periodic table can be worked out from the number of the group. For transition metals the charge on the ion is shown by the Roman numeral in the name of the compound, for example iron(II) sulfate contains Fe²⁺. In the examination you will have a data sheet showing the charges of ions.

● Some ions are made up of more than one element, for example carbonate ions are CO₃²⁻ and hydroxide ions are OH⁻. If we need to multiply these ions to write a formula we use brackets. The formula of calcium carbonate is CaCO₃, and the formula of calcium hydroxide is Ca(OH)₂.

▷ **1** *Write the formula for each of these compounds:*
   calcium fluoride, sodium sulfate, magnesium nitrate, copper(II) chloride, iron(III) hydroxide.

AQA Examiner's tip

Do not forget that ionic compounds are giant structures. The formula of an ionic compound is the simplest ratio of the ions in the compound and does not represent a molecule.

◢ **Bump up your grade**

Make sure you can write the correct formula for any compound from the ions on the data sheet.

Student Book
pages 88–89 **C2**

1.4 Covalent bonding

- The atoms of non-metals need to gain electrons to achieve stable electronic structures. They can do this by sharing electrons with other atoms. Each shared pair of electrons strongly attracts the two atoms, forming a covalent bond. Substances that have atoms held together by covalent bonding are called molecules.

- Atoms of elements in Group 7 need to gain one electron and so form a single covalent bond. Atoms of elements in Group 6 need to gain two electrons and so form two covalent bonds. Atoms of elements in Group 5 can form three bonds and those in Group 4 can form four bonds.

- A covalent bond acts only between the two atoms it bonds to each other, and so many covalently bonded substances consist of small molecules. Some atoms that can form several bonds, like carbon, can join together in giant covalent structures. These giant covalent structures are sometimes referred to as macromolecules.

Key points

- A covalent bond is formed when two atoms share a pair of electrons.

- The number of covalent bonds an atom forms depends on the number of electrons it needs to achieve a stable electronic structure.

- Many substances containing covalent bonds consist of simple molecules, but some have giant covalent structures.

AQA *Examiner's tip*

Covalent bonds join atoms together to form molecules. You should only use the word molecule when describing substances that are covalently bonded.

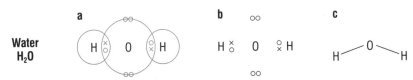

Water
H_2O

We can represent a covalent compound by showing electrons or using lines for covalent bonds

> 1 *Draw diagrams using symbols and lines to show the covalent bonds in: chlorine Cl_2, hydrogen chloride HCl, hydrogen sulfide H_2S, oxygen O_2, and carbon dioxide CO_2.*

Student Book
pages 90–91 **C2**

1.5 Metals

- The atoms in a metallic element are all the same size. They form giant structures in which layers of atoms are arranged in regular patterns. You can make models of metal structures by putting lots of small same-sized spheres like marbles together.

Key points

- The atoms in metals are closely packed together and arranged in regular layers.

- The electrons in the highest energy level are delocalised. The strong electrostatic forces between these electrons and the positively charged metal ions hold the metal together. **[H]**

> 1 *How are the atoms arranged in a metal?*

Metallic bonding

When metal atoms pack together the electrons in the highest energy level (the outer electrons) delocalise and can move freely between atoms. This produces a lattice of positive ions in a 'sea' of moving electrons. The **delocalised electrons** strongly attract the positive ions and hold the giant structure together.

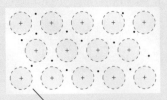

The 'sea' of delocalised electrons

> 2 *What forces hold metal atoms in place in their giant structures?*

Key word: delocalised electron

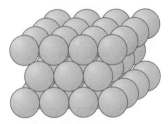

The close-packed arrangement of copper atoms in copper metal

1 What is a compound?

2 a Which electrons in an atom are involved in bonding?

b What happens to the electrons in atoms when ionic bonds are formed?

c What happens to electrons in atoms when covalent bonds are formed?

3 a Why do the elements in Group 1 form ions with a single positive charge?

b Why do the elements in Group 7 form ions with a single negative charge?

4 Which of the following substances are made of molecules?
KCl, H_2O, C_2H_6, MgO, CO_2, $NaNO_3$.

5 Why can the structure of a metallic element like copper be represented by lots of small spheres the same size packed together?

6 Write the correct formula for each of the following: lithium chloride, sodium oxide, calcium fluoride, magnesium hydroxide, sodium sulfate, calcium nitrate.

7 Why do ionic compounds have giant structures?

8 Draw a dot and cross diagram to show the bonding in methane, CH_4.

9 Draw diagrams using symbols and lines to show the covalent bonds in F_2, O_2, HBr, H_2O, NH_3.

10 Draw dot and cross diagrams to show what happens when a potassium atom reacts with a fluorine atom.

11 Explain why silicon (in Group 4) has a giant structure.

12 Explain how the atoms in a piece of sodium metal are held together.

[H]

Chapter checklist		✓ ✓ ✓
Tick when you have:		
reviewed it after your lesson	✓ ☐ ☐	Chemical bonding ☐ ☐ ☐
revised once – some questions right	✓ ✓ ☐	Ionic bonding ☐ ☐ ☐
revised twice – all questions right	✓ ✓ ✓	Formulae of ionic compounds ☐ ☐ ☐
Move on to another topic when you have all three ticks		Covalent bonding ☐ ☐ ☐
		Metals ☐ ☐ ☐

Student Book
pages 94–95 **C2**

2.1 Giant ionic structures

Key points

- Ionic compounds have giant structures in which many strong electrostatic forces hold the ions together. This means they are solids at room temperature. A lot of energy is needed to overcome the ionic bonds to melt the solids. Therefore ionic compounds have high melting points and high boiling points.

Key points

- Ionic compounds have high melting points and they are all solids at room temperature.

- Ionic compounds will conduct electricity when we melt them or dissolve them in water. Their ions can then move freely and can carry charge through the liquid.

▐▶ **1** *Why do ionic solids have high melting points?*

- However, when an ionic compound has been melted the ions are free to move. This allows them to carry electrical charge, so the liquids conduct electricity. Some ionic solids dissolve in water because water molecules can split up the lattice. The ions are free to move in the solutions and so they also conduct electricity.

▐▶ **2** *Why can ionic substances conduct electricity when molten or when dissolved in water?*

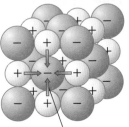

The attractive forces in an ionic compound are very strong

Strong electrostatic forces of attraction called ionic bonds

AQA *Examiner's tip*

Ionic compounds cannot conduct electricity when solid because the ions can only vibrate about fixed positions; they cannot move around. The compound must be melted or dissolved in water for the ions to be able to move about freely.

Student Book
pages 96–97 **C2**

2.2 Simple molecules

Key points

- Substances made up of simple molecules have low melting points and boiling points.

- Simple molecules have no overall charge, so they cannot carry electrical charge and do not conduct electricity.

- The weak intermolecular forces between simple molecules are why substances made of simple molecules have low melting points and boiling points. [H]

- The atoms within a molecule are held together by strong covalent bonds. These bonds act only between the atoms within the molecule, and so simple molecules have little attraction for each other. Substances made of simple molecules have relatively low melting points and boiling points. They do not conduct electricity because molecules have no overall charge and so cannot carry electrical charge.

▐▶ **1** *Why does petrol not conduct electricity?*

Intermolecular forces

The forces of attraction between molecules, called **intermolecular forces**, are weak. These forces are overcome when a molecular substance melts or boils. This means that substances made of small molecules have low melting and boiling points. Those with the smallest molecules, like H_2, Cl_2 and CH_4, have the weakest intermolecular forces and are gases at room temperature. Larger molecules have stronger attractions and so may be liquids at room temperature, like Br_2 and C_6H_{14}, or solids with low melting points, like I_2.

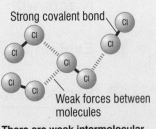

Strong covalent bond

Weak forces between molecules

There are weak intermolecular forces between chlorine molecules

▐▶ **2** *Why are substances with large molecules more likely to be liquids or solids at room temperature?*

Key word: intermolecular force

2.3 Giant covalent structures

Key points

- Covalently bonded substances with giant structures have very high melting points.
- Diamond is a form of carbon whose atoms each form four covalent bonds.
- Graphite is another form of carbon where the carbon atoms form layers that can slide over each other.
- Graphite can conduct electricity because of the delocalised electrons in its structure. **[H]**
- Carbon also exists as fullerenes. **[H]**

- Atoms of some elements can form several covalent bonds. These atoms can join together in **giant covalent structures** (sometimes called **macromolecules**). Every atom in the structure is joined to several other atoms by strong covalent bonds. It takes an enormous amount of energy to break down the lattice and so these substances have very high melting points.

▶ **1** *Why do substances with giant covalent structures have very high melting points?*

- Diamond is a form of carbon that has a regular three-dimensional giant structure. Every carbon atom is covalently bonded to four other carbon atoms. This makes diamond hard and transparent. The compound silicon dioxide (silica) has a similar structure.
- Graphite is a form of carbon in which the atoms are covalently bonded to three other carbon atoms in giant flat two-dimensional layers. There are no covalent bonds between the layers and so they slide over each other, making graphite slippery and grey.

▶ **2** *Give two similarities and two differences between diamond and graphite.*

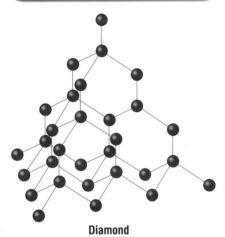

Diamond

The structure of diamond

Bonding in graphite and fullerenes

In graphite each carbon atom bonds covalently to three other carbon atoms forming a flat sheet of hexagons. One electron from each carbon atom is delocalised, rather like electrons in a metal. These **delocalised electrons** allow graphite to conduct heat and electricity.

There are only weak intermolecular forces between the layers in graphite, so the layers can slide over each other quite easily.

Fullerenes are large molecules formed from hexagonal rings of carbon atoms. The rings join together to form cage-like shapes with different numbers of carbon atoms, some of which are nano-sized. Scientists are finding many applications for fullerenes, including drug delivery into the body, lubricants, catalysts and reinforcing materials.

▶ **3** *Give two similarities and one difference between graphite and fullerenes.*

Higher

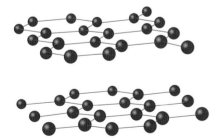

Graphite

The giant structure of graphite. When you write with a pencil, some layers of carbon atoms slide off the 'lead' and are left on the paper.

AQA **Examiner's tip**

Diamond and graphite both have very high melting points because they are both giant covalent structures.

Bump up your grade

If you are taking the higher paper, you should be able to explain the differences in the properties of graphite and diamond in terms of intermolecular forces and delocalised electrons.

Key words: giant covalent structure, macromolecule, fullerene

2.4 Giant metallic structures

- Metal atoms are arranged in layers. When a force is applied the layers of atoms can slide over each other. They can move into a new position without breaking apart, so the metal bends or stretches into a new shape. This means that metals are useful for making wires, rods and sheet materials.

▸ **1** *Why can metals be made into wires?*

- Alloys are mixtures of metals or metals mixed with other elements. The different sized atoms in the mixture distort the layers in the metal structure and make it more difficult for them to slide over each other. This makes alloys harder than pure metals.
- **Shape memory alloys** can be bent or deformed into a different shape. When they are heated they return to their original shape. They can be used in many ways, for example as dental braces.

▸ **2** *Give two reasons why alloys can be more useful than pure metals.*

Key points

- When we bend and shape metals the layers of atoms in the giant metallic structure slide over each other.
- Alloys are mixtures of metals and are harder than pure metals because the layers in the structure are distorted.
- If a shape-memory alloy is deformed, it can return to its original shape on heating.
- Delocalised electrons in metals enable metals to conduct heat and electricity well. **[H]**

Metal structures

Metal structures have delocalised electrons. Metals are good conductors of heat and electricity because the delocalised electrons move throughout the giant metallic lattice and can transfer energy quickly.

▸ **3** *Why are metals good conductors of electricity?*

Key word: shape memory alloy

Iron

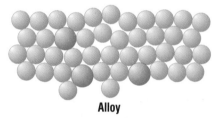

Alloy

The atoms in pure iron are arranged in layers that can easily slide over each other. In alloys the layers cannot slide so easily because atoms of other elements change the regular structure.

2.5 The properties of polymers

- The properties of a polymer depend on the monomers used to make it, and the conditions we use to carry out the reaction. Poly(propene) is made from propene and softens at a higher temperature than poly(ethene), which is made from ethene. Low density (LD) poly(ethene) and high density (HD) poly(ethene) are made using different catalysts and different reaction conditions. HD poly(ethene) has a higher softening temperature and is stronger than LD poly(ethene).

▸ **1** *Why do LD and HD poly(ethene) have different properties?*

- Poly(ethene) is an example of a **thermosoftening polymer**. It is made up of individual polymer chains that are tangled together. When it is heated it becomes soft and hardens again when it cools. This means it can be heated to mould it into shape and it can be remoulded by heating it again.
- Other polymers called **thermosetting polymers** do not melt or soften when we heat them. These polymers set hard when they are first moulded because strong covalent bonds form cross-links between their polymer chains. The strong bonds hold the polymer chains in position.

Key points

- The properties of polymers depend on the monomers used to make them.
- Changing reaction conditions can also change the properties of the polymer that is produced.
- Thermosoftening polymers soften or melt easily when heated.
- Thermosetting polymers do not soften or melt when heated.

The strands of spaghetti are like the polymer molecules of a themosoftening polymer

Electrical sockets are made of thermosetting plastics

▥▶ **2** *What is the main difference in the structures of thermosoftening and thermosetting polymers?*

Bonding in polymers

In thermosoftening polymers the forces between the polymer chains are weak. When we heat the polymer, these weak intermolecular forces are broken and the polymer becomes soft. When the polymer cools down, the intermolecular forces bring the polymer molecules back together so the polymer hardens again.

▥▶ **3** *What allows thermosoftening polymers to be remoulded?*

AQA Examiner's tip

You should be able to recognise the type of polymer from a diagram of its structure or a description of its properties. Thermosetting polymers have covalent bonds linking the chains and do not soften when heated.

Key words: thermosoftening polymer, thermosetting polymer

Higher

Student Book
pages 104–105

C2

2.6 Nanoscience

Key points

- Nanoscience is the study of small particles that are between 1 and 100 nanometres in size.
- Nanoparticles behave differently from the bulk materials they are made from.
- Developments in nanoscience are exciting but will need more research into possible issues that might arise from increased use.

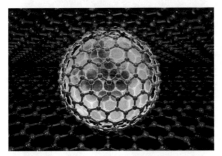

Nanocages can carry drugs inside them

- **Nanoscience** is a new and exciting area of science. When atoms are arranged into very small particles they behave differently to ordinary materials made of the same atoms. A nanometre is one billionth of a metre (or 10^{-9} m) and nanoparticles are a few nanometres in size. They contain a few hundred atoms arranged in a particular way. Their very small sizes give them very large surface areas and new properties that can make them very useful materials.

▥▶ **1** *What is a nanoparticle?*

- Nanotechnology uses nanoparticles as highly selective sensors, very efficient catalysts, new coatings, new cosmetics such as sun screens and deodorants, and to give construction materials special properties.
- If nanoparticles are used more and more there will be a greater risk of them finding their way into the air and into our bodies. This could have unpredictable consequences for our health and the environment. More research needs to be done to find out their effects.

▥▶ **2** *Scientists have developed a new deodorant containing nanoparticles. What should be done before it is sold for people to use?*

Key word: nanoscience

1 Why does it take a lot of energy to melt sodium chloride?

2 Why are compounds like methane, CH_4, and ammonia, NH_3, gases at room temperature?

3 Polymers made from different monomers have different properties. Explain why.

4 Some dental braces are made from shape-memory alloys. What is meant by a 'shape-memory alloy'?

5 Explain why diamonds are very hard.

6 Why do ionic compounds need to be molten or in solution to conduct electricity?

7 Explain why a block of copper can be hammered into a sheet.

8 Silver nanoparticles are used in some socks to help prevent bad smells.

   a How are silver nanoparticles different from ordinary silver particles?

   b Suggest why a sock manufacturer would use nanoparticles instead of ordinary silver particles.

9 Explain why thermosetting polymers are often used to make handles for cooking pans.

10 Explain how the atoms in a metal are bonded to each other. [H]

11 Why can graphite conduct electricity? [H]

12 Explain what is meant by 'intermolecular forces'. [H]

13 C_{60} is a fullerene. What are fullerenes? [H]

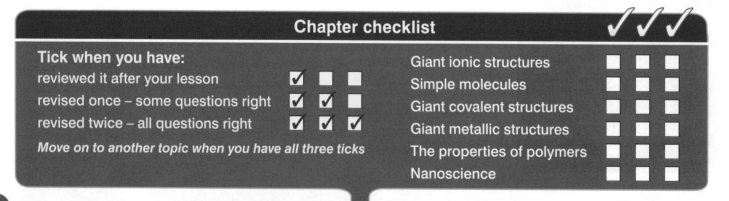

Chapter checklist ✓ ✓ ✓

Tick when you have:

reviewed it after your lesson ✓ ☐ ☐

revised once – some questions right ✓ ✓ ☐

revised twice – all questions right ✓ ✓ ✓

Move on to another topic when you have all three ticks

Giant ionic structures ☐ ☐ ☐

Simple molecules ☐ ☐ ☐

Giant covalent structures ☐ ☐ ☐

Giant metallic structures ☐ ☐ ☐

The properties of polymers ☐ ☐ ☐

Nanoscience ☐ ☐ ☐

3.1 The mass of atoms

- Protons and neutrons have the same mass and so the relative masses of a proton and a neutron are both one.
- The mass of an electron is very small compared with a proton or neutron, and so the mass of an atom is made up almost entirely of its protons and neutrons. The total number of protons and neutrons in an atom is called its **mass number**.

▧➡ **1** *Why do we count only protons and neutrons to calculate the mass number of an atom?*

- Atoms of the same element all have the same **atomic number**. The number of protons and electrons in an atom must always be the same, but there can be different numbers of neutrons.
- Atoms of the same element with different numbers of neutrons are called **isotopes**.
- The number of neutrons in an atom is equal to its mass number minus its atomic number. We can show the mass number and atomic number of an atom like this:

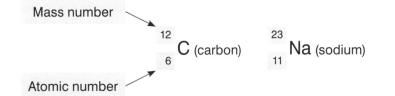

Mass number

$^{12}_{6}$C (carbon) $^{23}_{11}$Na (sodium)

Atomic number

- The number at the top is the mass number (which is larger than the atomic number, except for hydrogen, $^{1}_{1}$H).
- So this sodium atom sodium has 11 protons, 11 electrons and (23 − 11 =) 12 neutrons.

▧➡ **2** *How many protons, electrons and neutrons are there in an atom of $^{19}_{9}$F?*

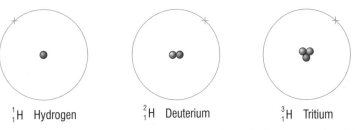

$^{1}_{1}$H Hydrogen $^{2}_{1}$H Deuterium $^{3}_{1}$H Tritium

The isotopes of hydrogen – they have identical chemical properties but different physical properties

▧➡ **3** *What are isotopes?*

Key words: mass number, atomic number, isotope

Key points

- The relative mass of protons and neutrons is 1.
- The atomic number of an atom is its number of protons (which equals its number of electrons).
- The mass number of an atom is the total number of protons and neutrons in its nucleus.
- Isotopes are atoms of the same element with different numbers of neutrons.

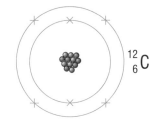

$^{12}_{6}$C

● Proton   Number of protons gives atomic number

● Neutron   Number of protons plus number of neutrons gives mass number

An atom of carbon

AQA *Examiner's tip*

Isotopes are atoms of the same element. They have the same chemical properties but they have different physical properties because of their different masses. Some isotopes are unstable and radioactive.

3.2 Masses of atoms and moles

- Atoms are much too small to weigh and so we use **relative atomic masses (A_r)** in calculations. Relative atomic masses are often shown in periodic tables. In the laboratory we usually weigh substances in grams. The relative atomic mass of an element in grams is called one **mole** of atoms of the element.

▐▶ **1** *What is the mass of one mole of sodium atoms?*

Key points

- We use relative atomic masses to compare the masses of atoms.

- The relative atomic mass of an element is an average value for the isotopes of an element. **[H]**

- We work out the relative formula mass of a compound by adding up the relative atomic masses of the elements in it.

- One mole of any substance is its relative formula mass in grams.

Relative atomic mass

We use an atom of $^{12}_{6}C$ as a standard atom and compare the masses of all other atoms with this. The relative atomic mass of an element (A_r) is an average value that depends on the isotopes the element contains. However, when rounded to a whole number it is often the same as the mass number of the main isotope of the element.

▐▶ **2** *Why is the relative atomic mass of chlorine not a whole number?*

- The **relative formula mass (M_r)** of a substance is found by adding up the relative atomic masses of the atoms in its formula.

Bump up your grade

Make sure you can calculate the relative formula mass (M_r) of a compound from its formula.

Maths skills

Worked example	**Answer**
Calculate the M_r of calcium chloride, $CaCl_2$	A_r of Ca = 40, A_r of Cl = 35.5, so $M_r = 40 + (35.5 \times 2) = 111$

AQA *Examiner's tip*

You do not have to remember relative atomic masses. In the exam you will have a data sheet with a periodic table that shows the relative atomic mass of each element.

▐▶ **3** *Calculate the relative formula mass (M_r) of sodium sulfate, Na_2SO_4. (Relative atomic masses: Na = 23, S = 32, O = 16).*

- The relative formula mass of a substance in grams is called one mole of that substance. Using moles of substances is useful when we need to work out how much of a substance reacts or how much product we will get.

Maths skills

Worked example	**Answer**
What is the mass of one mole of sodium hydroxide, NaOH?	A_r of Na = 23, A_r of O = 16, A_r of H = 1, so 1 mole NaOH = (23 + 16 + 1) g = 40 g

▐▶ **4** *What is the mass of one mole of magnesium carbonate, $MgCO_3$? (Relative atomic masses: Mg = 24, C = 12, O = 16).*

Key words: relative atomic mass, mole, relative formula mass

Student Book
pages 112–113 **C2**

3.3 Percentages and formulae

Key points

- The relative atomic masses of the elements in a compound and its formula can be used to work out its percentage composition.

- We can calculate empirical formulae given the masses or percentage composition of elements present. **[H]**

AQA Examiner's tip

When calculating an empirical formula it is helpful to set out your answer in a table. In the exam you should always show your working in calculations.

Bump up your grade

Practice calculating the percentage of an element in a compound from its formula.

If you are taking the Higher Tier paper you should be able to calculate the empirical formula of a compound with two or three elements from information about its percentage composition.

A small difference in the amount of metal in an ore might not seem very much. However, when millions of tonnes of ore are extracted and processed each year, it all adds up!

- We can calculate the percentage of any of the elements in a compound from the formula of the compound. Divide the relative atomic mass of the element by the relative formula mass of the compound and multiply the answer by 100 to convert it to a percentage. This can be useful when deciding if a compound is suitable for a particular purpose or to identify a compound.

Maths skills

Worked example

What is the percentage of carbon in carbon dioxide, CO_2?

Answer

A_r of C = 12, A_r of O = 16

M_r of CO_2 = 12 + (16 × 2) = 44

So percentage of carbon

= (12/44) × 100 = 27.3%

1 *What is the percentage of carbon in methane, CH_4? (A_r of C = 12, A_r of H = 1).*

Working out the formula of a compound from its percentage composition

The **empirical formula** is the simplest ratio of the atoms or ions in a compound. It is the formula used for ionic compounds, but for covalent compounds it is not always the same as the **molecular formula**. For example, the molecular formula of ethane is C_2H_6, but its empirical formula is CH_3.

We can calculate the empirical formula of a compound from its percentage composition:

- Divide the mass of each element in 100 g of the compound by its A_r to give the ratio of atoms.

- Then convert this to the simplest whole number ratio.

Maths skills

Worked example

What is the empirical formula of the hydrocarbon that contains 80% carbon?

Answer:

	Carbon	Hydrogen
Mass in 100 g of compound	80	20
Ratio of atoms or moles of atoms (mass/A_r)	80/12 = 6.67	20/1 = 20
Simplest ratio of atoms (divide by smallest)	6.67/6.67 = 1	20/6.67 = 3
Empirical formula	CH_3	

2 *What is the empirical formula of the compound that contains 70% iron and 30% oxygen? (A_r of Fe = 56, A_r of O = 16)*

Key words: empirical formula, molecular formula

3.4 Equations and calculations

Key points

- Balanced symbol equations tell us the number of moles of substances involved in a chemical reaction.   **[H]**

- We can use balanced symbol equations to calculate the masses of reactants and products in a chemical reaction.   **[H]**

AQA *Examiner's tip*

You can work in moles or you can use relative masses when doing calculations, but if you are asked to calculate a mass of a reactant or product do not forget to give the correct units in your answer.

Calculating masses from chemical equations

Chemical equations show the reactants and products of a reaction. When they are balanced they show the amounts of atoms, molecules or ions in the reaction. For example: $2Mg + O_2 \rightarrow 2MgO$ shows that two atoms of magnesium react with one molecule of oxygen to form two magnesium ions and two oxide ions.

If we work in moles, the equation tells us that two moles of magnesium atoms react with one mole of oxygen molecules to produce two moles of magnesium oxide.

This means that 48 g of magnesium react with 32 g of oxygen to give 80 g of magnesium oxide. (A_r of Mg = 24, A_r of O = 16)

Alternatively, if we work in relative masses from the equation: $(2 \times A_r$ of Mg$)+(2 \times A_r$ of O) gives $(2 \times M_r$ of MgO)

Converting this to grams it becomes 2×24 g Mg $+ 2 \times 16$ g O gives 2×40 g MgO or 48 g Mg $+ 32$ g O gives 80 g MgO (which is the same as when we used moles).

If we have 5 g of magnesium, we can work out the mass of magnesium oxide it will produce using ratios: 1 g Mg will produce 80/48 g MgO

so 5 g Mg will produce $5 \times 80/48$ g MgO = 8.33 g of MgO

If we use moles the calculation can be done like this:

1 mole of Mg produces 1 mole of MgO

5 g Mg = 5/24 mole of magnesium and so it will produce 5/24 mole of MgO.

The mass of 5/24 mole MgO = $5/24 \times 40$ g = 8.33 g of MgO

> **1** *Calculate the mass of calcium oxide that can be made from 10 g of calcium carbonate in the reaction:*
> $CaCO_3 \rightarrow CaO + CO_2$ *(A_r of Ca = 40, A_r of O = 16, A_r of C = 12)*

3.5 The yield of a chemical reaction

- The **yield** of a chemical process is how much you actually make. The **percentage yield** compares the amount made with the maximum amount that could be made, calculated as a percentage.

Key points

- The yield of a chemical reaction describes how much product is made.

- The percentage yield of a chemical reaction tells us how much product is made compared with the maximum amount that could be made.

- It is important to maximise yield and minimise energy wasted to conserve the Earth's limited resources and reduce pollution.

Calculating percentage yield

The percentage yield is calculated using this equation:

$$\text{Percentage yield} = \frac{\text{(amount of product collected}}{\text{maximum amount of product possible)}} \times 100\%$$

The maximum amount of product possible is calculated from the balanced equation for the reaction.

For example: A student collected 2.3 g of magnesium oxide from 2.0 g of magnesium.

Theoretically: $2Mg + O_2 \rightarrow 2MgO$, so 48 g of Mg should give 80 g of MgO, and so 2.0 g of Mg should give $2 \times 80/48 = 3.33$ g of MgO.

$$\text{Percentage yield} = \left(\frac{2.3}{3.33}\right) \times 100 = 69\%$$

▷ **1** *A student made 4.4g of calcium oxide from 4.0g of calcium. Calculate the percentage yield.* **[H]**

● When you actually do chemical reactions it is not usually possible to collect the amounts calculated from the chemical equations. Reactions may not go to completion, other reactions may happen and some product may be lost when it is separated or collected from the apparatus.

▷ **2** *Why is it not usually possible to get 100% yield from a chemical reaction?*

● Using reactions with high yields in industry helps to conserve resources and to reduce waste. Chemical processes should also waste as little energy as possible. Working in these ways helps to reduce pollution and makes production more sustainable.

▷ **3** *Why should chemical manufacturers use reactions with high yields?*

Key words: yield, percentage yield

Student Book
pages 118–119 **C2**

3.6 Reversible reactions

Key points

● In a reversible reaction the products of the reaction can react to make the original reactants.

● We can show a reversible reaction using the (reversible reaction) sign ⇌.

● If the products of a chemical reaction can react to produce the reactants, the reaction can go in both directions. This type of reaction is called a **reversible reaction** and is represented with the symbol ⇌. One arrow points in the forwards direction (to the right) and one backwards.

● An example of a reversible reaction is:

ammonium chloride ⇌ ammonia + hydrogen chloride

● When heated, ammonium chloride decomposes to produce ammonia and hydrogen chloride. When cooled, ammonia and hydrogen chloride react to produce ammonium chloride.

▷ **1** *What is a reversible reaction?*

Key word: reversible reaction

Heating ammonium chloride: an example of a reversible reaction

Student Book
pages 120–121 **C2**

3.7 Analysing substances

Key points

- Chemical analysis is used to identify food additives.
- Paper chromatography can be used to detect and identify artificial colours.

AQA Examiner's tip

You do not need to remember the names of specific food additives or what they are used for.

- Substances added to food to improve its qualities are called food additives. Food additives may be natural products or synthetic chemicals.
- Foods can be checked by chemical analysis to ensure only safe, permitted additives have been used. The methods used include paper **chromatography** and mass spectrometry.
- Paper chromatography can be used to analyse the artificial colours in food. A spot of colour is put onto paper and a solvent is allowed to move through the paper. The colours move different distances depending on their solubility.

▶ **1** *What method can be used to analyse the colours in food?*

Key word: chromatography

Student Book
pages 122–123 **C2**

3.8 Instrumental analysis

Key points

- Modern instrumental techniques provide fast, accurate and sensitive ways of analysing chemical substances.
- Compounds in a mixture can be separated using gas chromatography.
- Once separated, compounds can be identified using a mass spectrometer.
- The mass spectrometer can be used to find the relative molecular mass of a compound from its molecular ion peak. **[H]**

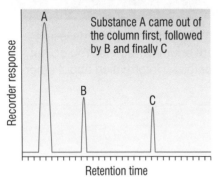

Substance A came out of the column first, followed by B and finally C

This is a gas chromatogram of a mixture of three different compounds

- Modern instrumental methods of analysis are rapid, accurate and sensitive, often using very small samples. Computers process the data from the instrument to give meaningful results almost instantly. The equipment is usually very expensive and special training is needed to use it.
- Samples for analysis are often mixtures that need to be separated so that the compounds can be identified. One way of doing this is to use **gas chromatography** linked to a **mass spectrometer**.
- In gas chromatography the mixture is carried by a gas through a long column packed with particles of a solid. The individual compounds travel at different speeds through the column and come out at different times. The amount of substance leaving the column at different times is recorded against time and shows the number of compounds in the mixture and their retention times. The **retention times** can be compared with the results for known compounds to help identify the compounds in the mixture.
- The output from the gas chromatography column can be linked directly to a mass spectrometer (GC–MS). The mass spectrometer gives further data that a computer can use quickly to identify the individual compounds.

▶ **1** *What is the main purpose of the gas chromatography column in GC–MS analysis?*

Measuring relative molecular masses

A mass spectrometer can give the relative molecular mass of a compound. For an individual compound the peak with the largest mass corresponds to an ion with just one electron removed. This peak is called the **molecular ion peak** and is furthest to the right on a mass spectrum.

▶ **2** *How is the relative molecular mass shown in a mass spectrum?*

Key words: gas chromatography, mass spectrometer, retention time, molecular ion peak

1 There are two main types of chlorine atom, $^{35}_{17}Cl$ and $^{37}_{17}Cl$.

    a What name is used for these two types of atom?

    b How is an atom of $^{35}_{17}Cl$ different from an atom of $^{37}_{17}Cl$?

2 Hydrogen and iodine react to make hydrogen iodide. The equation for the reaction is:

$$H_2 + I_2 \rightleftharpoons 2HI$$

What type of reaction is this?

3 What substances in foods can be detected by paper chromatography?

4 What is the relative formula mass of magnesium fluoride, MgF_2?

5 What is the mass of one mole of aluminium oxide, Al_2O_3?

6 What is the percentage by mass of copper in copper(II) carbonate, $CuCO_3$?

7 A student made some magnesium oxide by burning magnesium in air. The student obtained a yield of 55%. Suggest two reasons why the yield was less than 100%.

8 What is the empirical formula of vanadium oxide that contains 56% of vanadium?

    [H]

9 Calculate the mass of zinc chloride that you can make from 6.5 g of zinc.

$$Zn + 2HCl \rightarrow ZnCl_2 + H_2$$

    [H]

10 Calculate the percentage yield if 9.0 g $MgSO_4$ was made from 4.0 g MgO.   [H]

11 What information can be obtained from the molecular ion peak in a mass spectrum?

    [H]

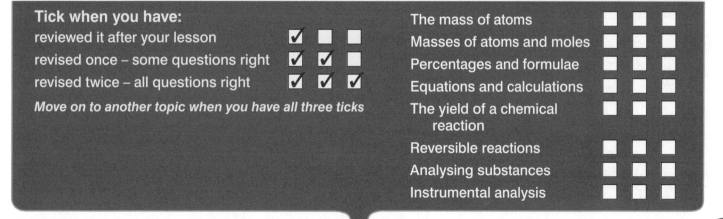

Chapter checklist

Tick when you have:
reviewed it after your lesson ✔ ☐ ☐
revised once – some questions right ✔ ✔ ☐
revised twice – all questions right ✔ ✔ ✔
Move on to another topic when you have all three ticks

The mass of atoms ☐ ☐ ☐
Masses of atoms and moles ☐ ☐ ☐
Percentages and formulae ☐ ☐ ☐
Equations and calculations ☐ ☐ ☐
The yield of a chemical reaction ☐ ☐ ☐
Reversible reactions ☐ ☐ ☐
Analysing substances ☐ ☐ ☐
Instrumental analysis ☐ ☐ ☐

Student Book
pages 126–127 **C2**

4.1 How fast?

- The **rate** of a reaction measures the speed of a reaction or how fast it is. The rate can be found by measuring how much of a reactant is used, or how much of a product is formed, and the time taken.
- Alternatively the rate can be found by measuring the time taken for a certain amount of reactant to be used or product to be formed. These methods give the average rate for the time measured.

$$\text{Rate of reaction} = \frac{\text{amount of reactant used}}{\text{time}} \quad \text{OR} \quad \frac{\text{amount of product formed}}{\text{time}}$$

- An average rate can also be found by measuring the time it takes for a certain amount of solid to appear in a solution. If a gas is given off in the reaction, its average rate can be found by measuring the time taken to collect a certain amount of gas.

▶ **1** *What two types of measurement must be made to find the average rate of a reaction?*

- The rate of a reaction at any given time can be found from the **gradient,** or slope, of the line on a graph of amount of reactant or product against time. The steeper the gradient is, the faster the reaction is at that time.
- A graph can be produced by measuring the mass of gas released or the volume of gas produced at intervals of time. Other possible ways include measuring changes in the colour, concentration, or pH of a reaction mixture over time.

▶ **2** *How can we use a graph of amount of product against time to tell us the rate of the reaction at a given time?*

Key word: gradient

Key points

- We can find the rate of a chemical reaction by measuring the amount of reactants used up over time or by measuring the amount of products made over time.
- The gradient or slope of the line on a graph of amount of reactant or product against time tells us the rate of reaction at that time. The steeper the gradient, the faster the reaction.

AQA *Examiner's tip*

The faster the rate, the shorter the time it takes for the reaction to finish. So rate is inversely proportional to time.

Student Book
pages 128–129 **C2**

4.2 Collision theory and surface area

- The **collision theory** states that reactions can only happen if particles collide. However, just colliding is not enough. The particles must collide with enough energy to change into new substances. The minimum energy they need to react is called the **activation energy**.

▶ **1** *What do we call the minimum energy needed for particles to react?*

- Factors that increase the chance of collisions, or the energy of the particles, will increase the rate of the reaction.
  Increasing the:
  - temperature,
  - concentration of solutions,
  - pressure of gases,
  - surface area of solids, and
  - using a catalyst
  will increase the rate of a reaction.

▶ **2** *List the factors that increase the rate of a reaction.*

Key points

- Particles must collide with a certain amount of energy before they can react.
- The minimum amount of energy that particles must have in order to react is called the activation energy.
- The rate of a chemical reaction increases if the surface area of any solid reactants is increased. This increases the frequency of collisions between reacting particles.

AQA *Examiner's tip*

Increasing the surface area means making the pieces smaller. More surface area produces more frequent collisions and so the rate of reaction is faster with powders than with larger pieces of solid.

- Breaking large pieces of a solid into smaller pieces exposes new surfaces and so increases the surface area. This means there are more collisions in the same time. So a powder reacts faster than large lumps of a substance. The finer the powder the faster the reaction.

▶ **3** *Why do powders react faster than large pieces of solid?*

Bump up your grade

Be careful with your use of language: increasing the surface area of a solid increases the frequency of the collisions. This means there are more collisions in the same time and this increases the rate of reaction. It is not enough to just write 'more collisions'.

Key words: collision theory, activation energy

Student Book pages 130–131 **C2**

4.3 The effect of temperature

Key points

- Reactions happen more quickly as the temperature increases.

- Increasing the temperature increases the rate of reaction because particles collide more frequently and more energetically.

- At a higher temperature more of the collisions result in a reaction because a higher proportion of particles have energy greater than the activation energy.

- Increasing the temperature increases the speed of the particles in a reaction mixture. This means they collide more often, which increases the rate of reaction. As well as colliding more frequently they collide with more energy, which also increases the rate of reaction.

- Therefore, a small change in temperature has a large effect on reaction rates. At ordinary temperatures a rise of 10 °C will roughly double the rate of many reactions, so they go twice as fast. A decrease in temperature will slow reactions down, and a decrease of 10 °C will double the time that many reactions take. This is why we refrigerate or freeze food so it stays fresh for longer.

▶ **1** *Why does a small change in temperature have a large effect on the rate of reaction?*

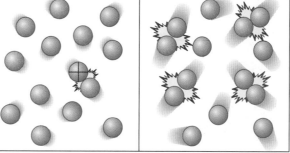

Cold – slow movement, less frequent collisions, little energy

Hot – fast movement, more frequent collisions, more energy

More frequent collisions, with more energy – both of these factors increase the rate of a chemical reaction caused by increasing the temperature.

AQA *Examiner's tip*

Increasing the temperature has a large effect on the rate of a reaction because it increases the frequency of collisions and it increases the energy of the particles.

Bump up your grade

Make sure you can explain the effect of temperature on the rate of a reaction in terms of particle collisions and activation energy.

Student Book
pages 132–133 **C2**

4.4 The effect of concentration or pressure

Student Book
pages 134–135 **C2**

Key points

- Increasing the concentration of reactants in solutions increases the frequency of collisions between particles, and so increases the rate of reaction.
- Increasing the pressure of reacting gases also increases the frequency of collisions and so increases the rate of reaction.

Bump up your grade

Make sure you can explain the effect of concentration on the rate of a reaction in terms of particle collisions. You should also be able to explain the effect of pressure on reactions of gases.

- The particles in a solution are moving around randomly. If the concentration of a solution is increased there are more particles dissolved in the same volume. This means the dissolved particles are closer together and so they collide more often.
- Increasing the concentration of a reactant therefore increases the rate of a reaction because the particles collide more frequently.

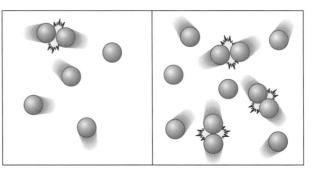

Low concentration/low pressure

High concentration/high pressure

Increasing concentration and pressure mean that particles are closer together. This increases the frequency of collisions between particles, so the reaction rate increases.

▶ **1** *Why do reactions in solutions go faster at higher concentrations?*

- In a similar way, increasing the pressure of a gas puts more molecules into the same volume, and so they collide more frequently. This increases the rate of reactions that have gases as reactants.

▶ **2** *Why does increasing the pressure increase the rate of a reaction of two gases?*

4.5 The effect of catalysts

Key points

- A catalyst speeds up the rate of a chemical reaction.
- A catalyst is not used up during a chemical reaction.
- Different catalysts are needed for different reactions.

Examiner's tip

You may have studied some specific examples of catalysts but you do not need to remember their names or the reactions they catalyse.

- **Catalysts** change the rates of chemical reactions. Most catalysts are used to speed up reactions. Catalysts that speed up reactions lower the activation energy of the reaction so that more of the collisions result in a reaction.
- Although the catalyst changes the rate of the reaction it is not used up. The catalyst is left at the end of the reaction and so it can be used over and over again.

▶ **1** *Why can catalysts be used over and over again?*

- Catalysts that are solids are used in forms that have large surface areas to make them as effective as possible.
- Catalysts often work with only one type of reaction and so different reactions need different catalysts.

▶ **2** *Why do different reactions need different catalysts?*

Key word: catalyst

Student Book
pages 136–137 **C2**

4.6 Catalysts in action

- Some catalysts are expensive but they can be economical because they do not need replacing very often. They are used in many industrial processes because they can reduce the energy and the time needed for reactions. This helps to reduce costs and reduce impacts on the environment. If fossil fuels are burned to provide energy for industrial reactions, using catalysts will help to conserve resources and reduce pollution.

▸ **1** *What are the benefits of using catalysts in industrial processes?*

- Many of the catalysts used in industry involve transition metals and their compounds. Some of these metals and their compounds are toxic and may cause harm if they get into the environment.

▸ **2** *Give one disadvantage of transition metal catalysts.*

- Finding new and better catalysts is a major area of research for the chemical industry. Nanoparticles offer exciting possibilities for developing new, highly efficient catalysts. Enzymes are biological catalysts that work at ordinary temperatures. If they can replace more traditional catalysts they will reduce energy costs even further.

▸ **3** *What two areas of research offer possibilities for new or better catalysts?*

Key points

- Catalysts are used in industry to increase the rate of reactions and reduce energy costs.
- Traditional catalysts are often transition metals or their compounds.
- Modern catalysts are being developed in industry which result in less waste and are safer for the environment.

AQA Examiner's tip

You should be aware of some of the issues involved in the use of catalysts but you do not need to remember the names of any specific examples.

Student Book
pages 138–139 **C2**

4.7 Exothermic and endothermic reactions

- When chemical reactions take place energy is transferred as bonds are broken and made. Reactions that transfer energy to the surroundings are called **exothermic** reactions. The energy transferred often heats up the surroundings and so the temperature increases.

Exothermic reactions include:
- combustion, such as burning fuels,
- oxidation reactions, such as respiration, and
- neutralisation reactions involving acids and bases.

▸ **1** *How can you tell that burning natural gas is an exothermic reaction?*

- **Endothermic** reactions take in energy from the surroundings.
- Some cause a decrease in temperature and others require a supply of energy. When some solid compounds are mixed with water, the temperature decreases because endothermic changes happen as they dissolve.
- **Thermal decomposition** reactions need to be heated continuously to keep the reaction going.

▸ **2** *What are the two ways that show that a reaction is endothermic?*

Key words: exothermic, endothermic, thermal decomposition

Key points

- Energy may be transferred to or from the reacting substances in a reaction.
- A reaction in which energy is transferred from the reacting substances to their surroundings is called an exothermic reaction.
- A reaction in which energy is transferred to the reacting substances from their surroundings is called an endothermic reaction.

Bump up your grade

Make sure you can recognise a reaction as exothermic or endothermic from temperature changes provided.

Student Book
pages 140–141 **C2**

4.8 Energy and reversible reactions

Key points

- In reversible reactions, the reaction in one direction is exothermic and in the other direction it is endothermic.

- In any reversible reaction, the amount of energy released when the reaction goes in one direction is exactly equal to the energy absorbed when the reaction goes in the opposite direction.

- In reversible reactions, the forward and reverse reactions involve equal but opposite energy transfers. A reversible reaction that is exothermic in one direction must be endothermic in the other direction. The amount of energy released by the exothermic reaction exactly equals the amount taken in by the endothermic reaction.

- When blue copper sulfate crystals are heated the reaction is endothermic:

$$\text{blue crystals} \qquad \text{white powder}$$
$$CuSO_4 \cdot 5H_2O \; \rightleftharpoons \; CuSO_4 \quad +5H_2O$$
$$\textbf{hydrated} \qquad \textbf{anhydrous}$$
$$\text{copper sulfate} \qquad \text{copper sulfate}$$

▷ **1** *Why must blue copper sulfate be heated continuously to change it into anhydrous copper sulfate?*

- When water is added to anhydrous copper sulfate the reaction is exothermic.

▷ **2** *Why does adding water to anhydrous copper sulfate cause the mixture to get hot?*

Key words: hydrated, anhydrous

Student Book
pages 142–143 **C2**

4.9 Using energy transfers from reactions

Key points

- Exothermic changes can be used in hand warmers and self-heating cans.

- Endothermic changes can be used in instant cold packs for sports injuries.

- Exothermic reactions can be used to heat things. Hand warmers and self-heating cans use exothermic reactions. In some hand warmers and cans the reactants are used up and so they cannot be used again. They use reactions such as the oxidation of iron or the reaction of calcium oxide with water. Other hand warmers use a reversible reaction such as the crystallisation of a salt. Once used, the pack can be heated in boiling water to re-dissolve the salt. These can be re-used many times.

▷ **1** *Suggest one advantage and one disadvantage of a re-usable hand warmer compared with a single use hand warmer.*

- Endothermic changes can be used to cool things. Some chemical cold packs contain ammonium nitrate and water that are kept separated. When mixed together the ammonium nitrate dissolves and takes in energy from the surroundings. The cold pack can be used on sports injuries or to cool drinks. The reaction is reversible but not in the pack and so this type of pack can be used only once.

▷ **2** *Suggest one advantage and one disadvantage of a chemical cold pack compared with using an ice pack.*

A reusable hand warmer based on recrystallisation

Instant cold packs can be applied to injuries

AQA Examiner's tip

You should know some examples of types of application of exothermic and endothermic reactions such as hand warmers and cold packs, but you do not need to remember the details of how they work or the reactions that are used. However, you may be asked to evaluate information that you are given about specific applications.

1 Pieces of zinc react with dilute hydrochloric acid:

$$Zn(s) + 2HCl(aq) \rightarrow ZnCl_2(aq) + H_2(g)$$

In what ways could you increase the rate of the reaction between zinc and hydrochloric acid?

2 How can you find the rate of a reaction from a graph of mass of product against time?

3 What is meant by the 'activation energy' of a reaction?

4 Name two types of reaction that are exothermic.

5 Why must calcium carbonate be heated continuously to convert it into calcium oxide and carbon dioxide?

6 Nitrogen and oxygen react together to produce nitrogen oxide:

$$N_2(g) + O_2(g) \rightarrow 2NO(g)$$

What changes in conditions would increase the rate of this reaction?

7 Explain in terms of particles why increasing the concentration of a reactant increases the rate of the reaction.

8 Explain why increasing the temperature increases the rate of a reaction.

Chapter checklist ✓✓✓

Tick when you have:				How fast?	☐	☐	☐
reviewed it after your lesson	✓	☐	☐	Collision theory and surface area	☐	☐	☐
revised once – some questions right	✓	✓	☐	The effect of temperature	☐	☐	☐
revised twice – all questions right	✓	✓	✓	The effect of concentration or pressure	☐	☐	☐
Move on to another topic when you have all three ticks				The effect of catalysts	☐	☐	☐
				Catalysts in action	☐	☐	☐
				Exothermic and endothermic reactions	☐	☐	☐
				Energy and reversible reactions	☐	☐	☐
				Using energy transfers from reactions	☐	☐	☐

5.1 Acids and alkalis

- Pure water is **neutral** and has a pH value of 7.
- **Acids** are substances that produce hydrogen ions, H⁺(aq), when they are added to water.
- When we dissolve a substance in water we make an **aqueous solution**.
- The **state symbol** (aq) shows that the ions are in aqueous solution. Hydrogen ions make solutions acidic and they have pH values of less than 7.

1 *Which ions are produced by acids when they are added to water?*

- **Bases** react with acids and neutralise them.
- **Alkalis** are bases that dissolve in water to make alkaline solutions. Alkalis produce hydroxide ions, OH⁻(aq), in the solution. Alkaline solutions have pH values greater than 7.

2 *What is an alkali?*

- The **pH scale** has values from 0 to 14. Solutions that are very acidic have low pH values of between 0 and 2. Solutions that are very alkaline have high pH values of 12 to 14.
- **Indicators** have different colours in acidic and alkaline solutions. **Universal indicator (UI)** and full-range indicators have different colours at different pH values.

3 *Which indicators can tell us the pH of a solution?*

Key words: neutral, acid, aqueous solution, state symbol, base, alkali, pH scale, universal indicator (UI)

Key points

- When acids are added to water they produce hydrogen ions, H⁺(aq), in the solution.
- Bases are substances that will neutralise acids.
- Alkalis dissolve in water to give hydroxide ions, OH⁻(aq), in the solution.
- The pH scale shows how acidic or alkaline a solution is.

AQA Examiner's tip

All alkalis are bases, and all bases neutralise acids, but only bases that dissolve in water are alkalis.

5.2 Making salts from metals or bases

- Acids will react with metals that are above hydrogen in the reactivity series.
- However, the reactions of acids with very reactive metals, such as sodium and potassium, are too violent to be done safely.
- When metals react with acids they produce a salt and hydrogen gas.

acid + metal → a **salt** + hydrogen
H₂SO₄(aq) + Zn(s) → ZnSO₄(aq) + H₂(g)

1 *Name a metal other than zinc that can safely react with an acid to produce a salt.*

- Metal oxides and metal hydroxides are bases. When an acid reacts with a base a **neutralisation** reaction takes place and a salt and water are produced.

acid + base → a salt + water
2HCl(aq) + MgO(s) → MgCl₂(aq) + H₂O(l)

Key points

- When an acid reacts with a base a neutralisation reaction takes place and produces a salt and water.
- Some salts can be made by the reaction of a metal with an acid. This reaction produces hydrogen gas as well as a salt.
- Salts can be crystallised from solutions by evaporating off water.

Learn the formulae of the three important acids HCl, HNO_3 and H_2SO_4 to help you to write the formulae of their salts. Remember that when they form salts hydrogen is lost from the acid so they form chlorides, nitrates and sulfates.

- These reactions can be used to make salts.
- A metal, or a base that is insoluble in water, is added a little at a time to the acid until all of the acid has reacted. The mixture is then filtered to remove the excess solid reactant, leaving a solution of the salt.
- The solid salt is made when water is evaporated from the solution so that it crystallises.

2 *Why do we add excess of the base when making a salt?*

- Chlorides are made from hydrochloric acid, nitrates from nitric acid and sulfates from sulfuric acid.

3 *Name the products when (a) nitric acid reacts with magnesium, (b) hydrochloric acid reacts with copper hydroxide.*

Key words: salt, neutralisation

Student Book pages 150–151 **C2**

5.3 Making salts from solutions

Key points

- When a soluble salt is made from an alkali and an acid, an indicator can be used to show when the reaction is complete.
- Insoluble salts can be made by reacting two solutions to produce a precipitate.
- Precipitation is an important way of removing some metal ions from industrial waste water.

You do not need to remember which salts are soluble or insoluble because you will be told about the solubility of salts in any exam questions.

- We can make soluble salts by reacting an acid and an alkali:

e.g. acid + alkali → salt + water
$HCl(aq) + NaOH(aq) \rightarrow NaCl(aq) + H_2O(l)$

- We can represent the neutralisation reaction between any acid and any alkali by this equation:

$$H^+(aq) + OH^-(aq) \rightarrow H_2O(l)$$

- There is no visible change when acids react with alkalis so we need to use an indicator or a pH meter to show when the reaction is complete. The solid salt can be obtained from the solution by crystallisation.

1 *What compound is produced in every neutralisation reaction?*

- Ammonia solution is an alkali that does not contain a metal. It reacts with acids to produce ammonium salts, such as ammonium nitrate, NH_4NO_3. Ammonium salts are used as fertilisers.
- We can make insoluble salts by mixing solutions of soluble salts that contain the ions needed. For example, we can make lead iodide by mixing solutions of lead nitrate and potassium iodide. The lead iodide forms a **precipitate** that can be filtered from the solution, washed with distilled water and dried.

$$Pb(NO_3)_2(aq) + 2KI(aq) \rightarrow PbI_2(s) + 2KNO_3(aq)$$

- Some pollutants, such as metal ions, can be removed from water by **precipitation**. The water is treated by adding substances that react with the pollutant metal ions dissolved in the water to form insoluble salts.

2 *Zinc carbonate is insoluble in water. What would happen when sodium carbonate solution is added to zinc sulfate solution?*

Key word: precipitate

Student Book
pages 152–153 **C2**

5.4 Electrolysis

- Electrolysis is the process that uses electricity to break down ionic compounds into elements.
- When electricity is passed through a molten ionic compound or a solution containing ions, electrolysis takes place.
- The substance that is broken down is called the **electrolyte**.

▶ **1** *What must be done to ionic compounds before they can be electrolysed?*

- The electrical circuit has two electrodes that make contact with the electrolyte. The electrodes are often made of an **inert** substance that does not react with the products.
- The ions in the electrolyte move to the electrodes where they are discharged to produce elements.
- Positively charged ions are attracted to the negative electrode where they form metals or hydrogen, depending on the ions in the electrolyte.
- Negatively charged ions are attracted to the positive electrode where they lose their charge to form non-metallic elements.

For example, when molten lead bromide is electrolysed, lead is produced at the negative electrode. At the same time bromine is produced at the positive electrode.

▶ **2** *Molten zinc chloride is electrolysed. Name the substances produced (a) at the positive electrode and (b) at the negative electrode.*

Key words: electrolyte, inert

Key points

- Electrolysis splits up a substance using electricity.
- Ionic compounds can only be electrolysed when they are molten or in solution because then their ions are free to move to the electrodes.
- In electrolysis, positive ions move to the negative electrode and negative ions move to the positive electrode.

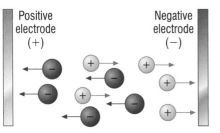

Positive electrode (+)   Negative electrode (−)

An ion always moves towards the oppositely charged electrode

Student Book
pages 154–155 **C2**

5.5 Changes at the electrodes

- When positively charged ions reach the negative electrode they gain electrons to become neutral atoms.
- Gaining electrons is called **reduction**, so the positive ions have been reduced. Ions with a single positive charge gain one electron and those with a 2+ charge gain 2 electrons.
- At the positive electrode, negative ions lose electrons to become neutral atoms. This is **oxidation**. Some non-metal atoms combine to form molecules, for example bromine forms Br_2.

▶ **1** *What type of change happens at the negative electrode when sodium ions become sodium atoms?*

Half equations

We can represent the changes at the electrodes by half equations. The half equations for lead bromide are:

At the negative electrode: $Pb^{2+} + 2e^- \rightarrow Pb$

At the positive electrode: $2Br^- \rightarrow Br_2 + 2e^-$

▶ **2** *Complete the half equation for the formation of chlorine at a positive electrode:* $2Cl^- \rightarrow \ldots + \ldots$

Key points

- Negative ions lose electrons and so are oxidised at the positive electrode.
- Positive ions gain electrons and so are reduced at the negative electrode.
- When aqueous solutions are electrolysed, oxygen gas is produced at the positive electrode unless the solution contains halide ions.
- When aqueous solutions are electrolysed, hydrogen gas is produced at the negative electrode unless the solution contains ions of a metal that is less reactive than hydrogen.

• Water contains hydrogen ions and hydroxide ions.

• When solutions of ions in water are electrolysed, hydrogen may be produced at the negative electrode. This happens if the other positive ions in the solution are those of a metal more reactive than hydrogen.

• At the positive electrode oxygen is usually produced from aqueous solutions. However, if the solution contains a reasonably high concentration of a halide ion, then a halogen will be produced.

⮕ **3** *Name the products at (a) the positive and (b) the negative electrodes when aqueous copper sulfate solution is electrolysed using carbon electrodes.*

Key words: reduction, oxidation

5.6 The extraction of aluminium

• Aluminium is more reactive than carbon and so it must be extracted from its ore by electrolysis. Its ore contains aluminium oxide which must be purified and then melted so that it can be electrolysed. Aluminium oxide melts at over 2000 °C, which would need a lot of energy. Aluminium oxide is mixed with another ionic compound called cryolite, so that the mixture melts at about 850 °C. The mixture can be electrolysed at this lower temperature and produces aluminium and oxygen as the products.

⮕ **1** *Why is aluminium oxide mixed with cryolite in the electrolysis cell?*

• The overall reaction in the electrolysis cell is:

$$\text{aluminium oxide} \rightarrow \text{aluminium} + \text{oxygen}$$
$$2Al_2O_3(l) \rightarrow 4Al(l) + 3O_2(g)$$

• The cryolite remains in the cell and fresh aluminium oxide is added as aluminium and oxygen are produced.

• At the negative electrode aluminium ions are reduced to aluminium atoms by gaining electrons. The molten aluminium metal is collected from the bottom of the cell.

• At the positive electrode oxide ions are oxidised to oxygen atoms by losing electrons and the oxygen atoms form oxygen molecules.

⮕ **2** *What are the final products of the electrolysis cell?*

Half equations

At the negative electrode: $Al^{3+}(l) + 3e^- \rightarrow Al(l)$

At the positive electrode: $2O^{2-}(l) \rightarrow 2O_2(g) + 4e^-$

• The positive electrodes used in the cell are made of carbon. At the high temperature of the cell the oxygen reacts with the carbon electrodes to produce carbon dioxide. This means that the carbon electrodes gradually burn away and so they have to be replaced regularly.

Higher

Student Book
pages 158–159

C2

5.7 Electrolysis of brine

Key points

- When we electrolyse brine we get three products – chlorine gas, hydrogen gas and sodium hydroxide solution.
- The products are important reactants used in industry.

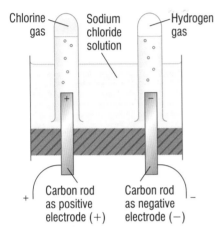

Electrolysis of sodium chloride solution

- Brine is a solution of sodium chloride in water. The solution contains sodium ions, $Na^+(aq)$, chloride ions, $Cl^-(aq)$, hydrogen ions, $H^+(aq)$, and hydroxide ions, $OH^-(aq)$. When brine is electrolysed hydrogen is produced at the negative electrode from the hydrogen ions. Chlorine is produced at the positive electrode from the chloride ions. This leaves a solution of sodium ions and hydroxide ions, $NaOH(aq)$.

▸ **1** *Why is hydrogen produced when sodium chloride solution is electrolysed?*

Half equations

The half equations for the reactions at the electrodes are:

At the positive electrode: $2Cl^- \rightarrow Cl_2 + 2e^-$

At the negative electrode: $2H^+ + 2e^- \rightarrow H_2$

- Sodium hydroxide is a strong alkali and has many uses including making soap, making paper, making bleach, neutralising acids and controlling pH.
- Chlorine is used to kill bacteria in drinking water and in swimming pools, and to make bleach, disinfectants and plastics.
- Hydrogen is used to make margarine and hydrochloric acid.

▸ **2** *Why is the electrolysis of brine an important industrial process?*

Student Book
pages 160–161

C2

5.8 Electroplating

Key points

- We can electroplate objects to improve their appearance, protect their surface, and to use smaller amounts of precious metals.
- The object to be electroplated is made the negative electrode in an electrolysis cell. The plating metal is made the positive electrode. The electrolyte contains ions of the plating metal.

AQA *Examiner's tip*

For electroplating the positive electrode is not inert – it produces ions of the metal used to plate the object.

Electroplating uses electrolysis to put a thin coating of metal onto an object. Gold, silver and chromium plating are often used. Electroplating can be done for several reasons that may include:

- to make the object look more attractive
- to protect a metal object from corroding
- to increase the hardness of a surface
- to reduce costs by using a thin layer of metal instead of the pure metal.

▸ **1** *Why are some knives, forks and spoons silver-plated?*

- For electroplating, the object to be plated is used as the negative electrode. The positive electrode is made from the plating metal. The electrolyte is a solution containing ions of the plating metal. At the positive electrode, atoms of the plating metal lose electrons to form metal ions which go into the solution. At the negative electrode, metal ions from the solution gain electrons to form metal atoms which are deposited on the object to be plated.

Half equations for nickel electroplating

At the positive nickel electrode: $Ni(s) \rightarrow Ni^{2+}(aq) + 2e^-$

At the negative electrode to be plated: $Ni^{2+}(aq) + 2e^- \rightarrow Ni(s)$

▸ **2** *Describe how you would silver plate a small piece of copper jewellery.*

1 Dilute nitric acid is added to sodium hydroxide solution.

   a What type of substance is sodium hydroxide?

   b What type of reaction happens?

   c Why is an indicator used to show when the reaction is complete?

   d Write a word equation for the reaction.

2 Describe the main steps to make zinc sulfate crystals from zinc oxide and dilute sulfuric acid.

3 Describe how you could make some insoluble lead sulfate from solutions of lead nitrate and sodium sulfate.

4 Why are some items of jewellery made of gold-plated nickel?

5 Name the products when sodium chloride solution is electrolysed and give one use for each.

6 Aluminium is manufactured from aluminium oxide, Al_2O_3, which is inexpensive.

   a Why is manufacturing aluminium an expensive process?

   b Why is cryolite used in the process to make aluminium?

7 Explain as fully as you can what happens at the electrodes when molten sodium chloride is electrolysed.

8 Write half equations for the reactions at the electrodes when magnesium chloride solution $MgCl_2$(aq) is electrolysed using carbon electrodes.   [H]

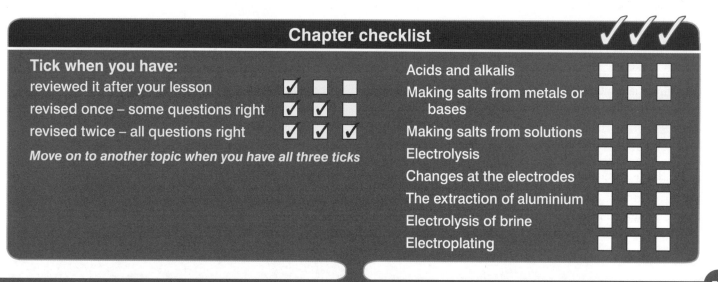

Chapter checklist	✓	✓	✓
Tick when you have:			
reviewed it after your lesson	☑	☐	☐
revised once – some questions right	☑	☑	☐
revised twice – all questions right	☑	☑	☑
Move on to another topic when you have all three ticks			
Acids and alkalis	☐	☐	☐
Making salts from metals or bases	☐	☐	☐
Making salts from solutions	☐	☐	☐
Electrolysis	☐	☐	☐
Changes at the electrodes	☐	☐	☐
The extraction of aluminium	☐	☐	☐
Electrolysis of brine	☐	☐	☐
Electroplating	☐	☐	☐

1 Lithium reacts with fluorine to produce lithium fluoride:

$$2Li(s) + F_2(g) \rightarrow 2LiF(s)$$

   a For each substance in the equation choose the type of bonding it has from this list:
ionic, covalent, metallic. *(3 marks)*

   b Which of the substances in the equation is made of small molecules? *(1 mark)*

   c Which of the substances in the equation would you expect to conduct electricity:
i when solid   **ii** when molten? *(2 marks)*

   d A lithium atom can be represented as shown:

     i   Draw a similar diagram to show a fluorine atom. *(1 mark)*

     ii   Use similar diagrams to show the bonding in lithium fluoride. *(4 marks)*

   e Lithium nanoparticles are used in some batteries.

     i   What is meant by the term nanoparticle? *(1 mark)*

     ii   Suggest **one** advantage of using lithium nanoparticles instead of normal
lithium. *(1 mark)*

   f Explain how the atoms are held together in solid lithium. **[H]** *(4 marks)*

2 Calcium hydrogenphosphate, $CaHPO_4$, is used as a dietary supplement in breakfast
cereals.

   a Calculate the formula mass, M_r, of $CaHPO_4$.
(Relative atomic masses: Ca = 40, H = 1, P = 31, O = 16) *(2 marks)*

   b Calculate the percentage of calcium in $CaHPO_4$. *(2 marks)*

   c Calcium carbonate, $CaCO_3$, is also used as a dietary supplement. Which compound
provides more calcium per 100 g? Show your working.
(Relative atomic mass of C = 12) *(2 marks)*

   d Calcium hydrogenphosphate contains atoms of the isotope $^{31}_{15}P$. Another isotope of
phosphorus is $^{32}_{15}P$.
Explain what is meant by the term isotope using these two types of phosphorus
atoms as examples. *(3 marks)*

   e An oxide of phosphorus contains 43.7% phosphorus. Calculate the empirical
formula of this oxide. **[H]** *(4 marks)*

3 Ammonia is made in industry from nitrogen and hydrogen. The reaction can be
represented by the equation:

$$N_2(g) + 3H_2(g) \rightleftharpoons 2NH_3(g)$$

   a What does the symbol $\rightleftharpoons$ tell you about this reaction? *(1 mark)*

   b Draw a dot and cross diagram to show the bonding in a molecule of ammonia.
(2 marks)

   c Ammonia dissolves in water and reacts to produce an alkaline solution.

$$NH_3(g) + H_2O(l) \rightarrow NH_4^+(aq) + OH^-(aq)$$

    How can you tell from the equation that the solution is alkaline? *(1 mark)*

AQA Examiner's tip

When drawing dot and
cross diagrams to show
bonding as in Q1 d you
need only show the outer
electrons of the atoms or
ions.

AQA Examiner's tip

In calculations, such as
in Q2 and Q3 e, always
show your working – if you
make a mistake you may
still get marks for showing
you know how to do the
calculation.

d The soluble salt ammonium nitrate can be made by reacting ammonia solution with dilute nitric acid. The reaction can be represented by the equation:

$$NH_4^+(aq) + OH^-(aq) + H^+(aq) + NO_3^-(aq) \rightarrow NH_4^+(aq) + NO_3^-(aq) + H_2O(l)$$

   i   Write this equation in its simplest form. *(1 mark)*

   ii What type of reaction is this? *(1 mark)*

   iii *In this question you will be assessed on using good English, organising information clearly and using specialist terms where appropriate.*
   Describe how you would make some ammonium nitrate crystals in the laboratory. You should include a risk assessment in your answer. *(6 marks)*

e The reaction can also be represented by this equation: **[H]**

$$NH_3(aq) + HNO_3(aq) \rightarrow NH_4NO_3(aq)$$

   i   Calculate the maximum mass of ammonium nitrate that can be made from 1.7 g of ammonia. (Relative atomic masses: H = 1, N = 14, O = 16) *(3 marks)*

   ii A student made 5.2 g of ammonium nitrate crystals from 1.7 g of ammonia. What was the percentage yield? *(2 marks)*

4 Some types of hand warmers use the reaction of iron with oxygen:

$$4Fe(s) + 3O_2(g) \rightarrow 2Fe_2O_3(s)$$

The hand warmers contain iron powder moistened with salt solution. The salt acts as a catalyst. When air is allowed into the mixture it reacts with the iron and the pack gets warm. The hand warmers can work for several hours.

a What type of reaction transfers energy to the surroundings? *(1 mark)*

b What is meant by a catalyst? *(2 marks)*

c Suggest **two** ways, other than increasing the temperature, that could be used to make the reaction in the hand warmer go faster. *(2 marks)*

5 A student electrolysed some sodium chloride solution using the apparatus shown in the diagram.

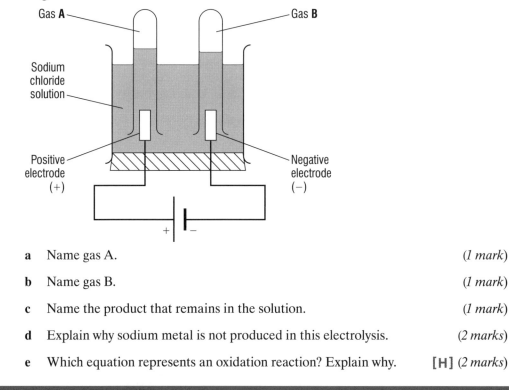

a Name gas A. *(1 mark)*

b Name gas B. *(1 mark)*

c Name the product that remains in the solution. *(1 mark)*

d Explain why sodium metal is not produced in this electrolysis. *(2 marks)*

e Which equation represents an oxidation reaction? Explain why. **[H]** *(2 marks)*

AQA *Examiner's tip*

In questions like 3 d iii that give marks for quality of written communication, plan your answer by writing brief notes of the main steps, make sure these are in a sensible order and then write your answer.

Student Book
pages 166–167 **P2**

1.1 Distance–time graphs

- We can use graphs to help us describe the motion of an object.
- A distance–time graph shows the distance of an object from a starting point (*y*-axis) against time taken (*x*-axis).
- The **speed** of an object is the distance travelled each second.
- The gradient of the line on a distance–time graph represents speed. The steeper the gradient, the greater the speed.
- If an object is stationary, the line on a distance–time graph is horizontal.
- If an object is moving at a constant speed, the line on a distance–time graph is a straight line that slopes upwards.

▶ **1 What is the SI unit of distance?**

- We can calculate the speed of an object using the equation:

$$\text{Speed in metres per second, m/s} = \frac{\text{distance travelled in metres, m}}{\text{time taken in seconds, s}}$$

▶ **2 What is the speed of a runner who covers 400 m in 50 s?**

Key word: speed

Key points

- The gradient of the line on a distance–time graph represents an object's speed.
- The steeper the line on a distance–time graph, the greater the speed it represents.
- Speed (m/s) = $\dfrac{\text{distance travelled (m)}}{\text{time taken (s)}}$

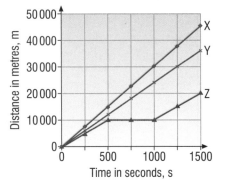

Comparing distance–time graphs

Student Book
pages 168–169 **P2**

1.2 Velocity and acceleration

- The **velocity** of an object is its speed in a given direction.
- If the object changes direction it changes velocity, even if its speed stays the same.
- If the velocity of an object changes, we say that it accelerates.

▶ **1 What is the difference between speed and velocity?**

- We can calculate **acceleration** using the equation:

$$a = \frac{v - u}{t}$$

Where:
a is the acceleration in metres per second squared, m/s²
v is the final velocity in metres per second, m/s
u is the initial velocity in metres per second, m/s
t is the time taken for the change in seconds, s.

▶ **2 What is the SI unit of acceleration?**

- If the value calculated for acceleration is negative, the body is decelerating – slowing down. A **deceleration** is the same as a **negative acceleration**.

Key words: velocity, acceleration, deceleration

Key points

- Velocity is speed in a given direction.
- Acceleration is the change of velocity per second.

$$a = \frac{v - u}{t}$$

Bump up your grade

Be sure to learn the units here carefully. Don't confuse m/s (unit of speed and velocity) and m/s² (unit of acceleration).

Student Book
pages 170–171

P2

1.3 More about velocity–time graphs

Key points

- If the line on a velocity–time graph is horizontal, the acceleration is zero.
- The gradient of a velocity–time graph represents acceleration.
- The area under the line on a velocity–time graph is the distance travelled. [H]

- A velocity–time graph shows the velocity of an object (y-axis) against time taken (x-axis).
- The gradient of the line on a velocity–time graph represents acceleration.
- The steeper the gradient, the greater the acceleration.
- If the line on a velocity–time graph is a horizontal, the acceleration is zero. Therefore the object is travelling at a steady speed.
- If the gradient of the line is negative, the object is decelerating.

Higher

The **area** under the line on a velocity–time graph represents the distance travelled in a given time. The bigger the area, the greater the distance travelled.

1 *What does a horizontal line on a velocity–time graph represent?*
2 *What would the velocity–time graph for a steadily decelerating object look like?*

Student Book
pages 172–173

P2

1.4 Using graphs

Key points

- The speed of an object is given by the gradient of the line on its distance–time graph. [H]
- The acceleration of an object is given by the gradient of the line on its velocity–time graph. [H]
- The distance travelled by an object is given by the area under the line of its velocity–time graph. [H]

AQA Examiner's tip

Take care not to confuse distance–time graphs and velocity–time graphs.

1 *What does an upwardly curving line represent on a:*
a *distance–time graph*
b *velocity–time graph?*

Higher

Using distance–time and velocity–time graphs

If you calculate the gradient of the line on a distance–time graph for an object, your answer will be the speed of the object.

If you calculate the gradient of the line on a velocity–time graph for an object, your answer will be the acceleration of the object.

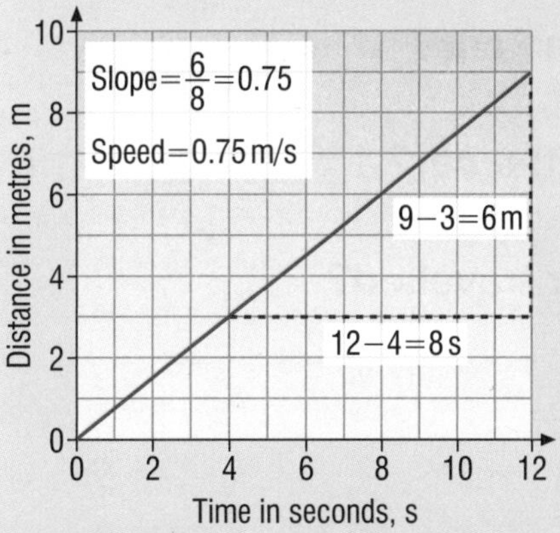

Finding the speed

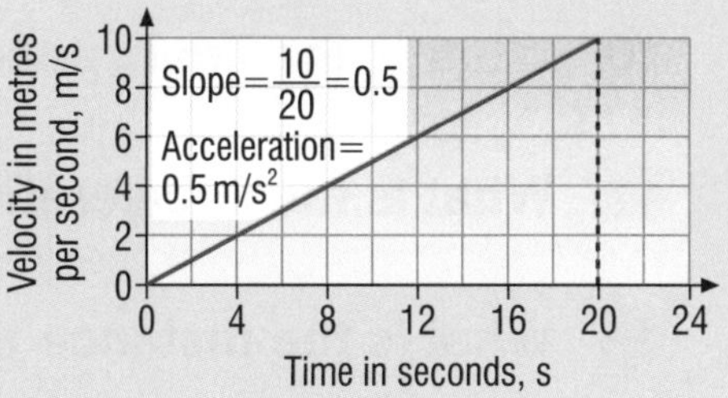

Finding the acceleration

Calculating the area under the line between two times on a velocity–time graph gives the distance travelled between those times.

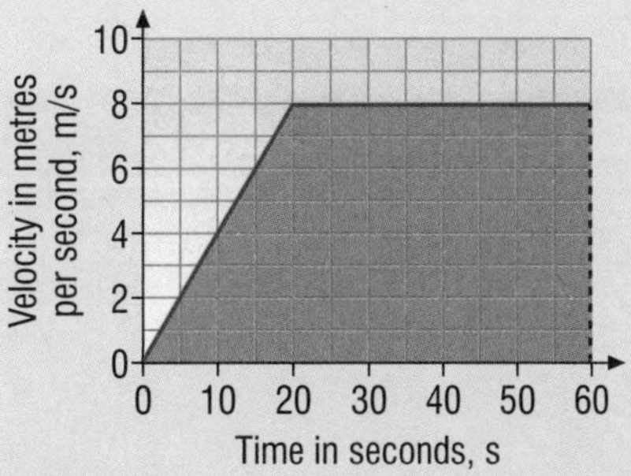

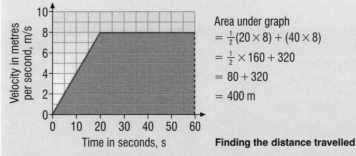

Area under graph
$= \frac{1}{2}(20 \times 8) + (40 \times 8)$
$= \frac{1}{2} \times 160 + 320$
$= 80 + 320$
$= 400$ m

Finding the distance travelled

Always use the numbers from the graph scales in any calculations.

1 What is the average speed, in m/s, of a car that completes a distance of 1.2 km in 1 minute?

2 What does the distance–time graph for a stationary object look like?

3 What quantity has the unit m/s²?

4 What does a negative value for acceleration mean?

5 What happens to the gradient of the line on a distance–time graph if the speed increases?

6 How can an object travelling at a steady speed be accelerating?

7 A car accelerates from rest to a speed of 40 m/s in 10 s. What is its acceleration?

8 What part of a velocity–time graph represents distance travelled?

The graph shows the motion of a car.

9 What is the initial speed of the car?

10 What is the final speed of the car?

11 What is the acceleration of the car? [H]

12 What is the distance the car travelled?

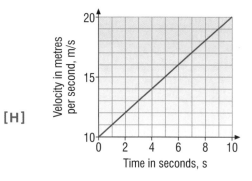

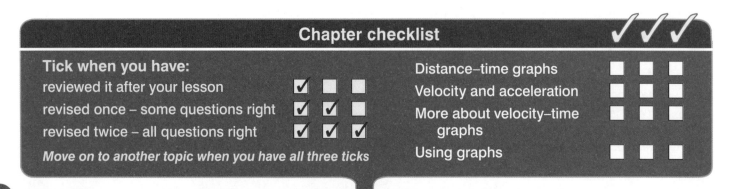

Chapter checklist		✓ ✓ ✓

Tick when you have:

reviewed it after your lesson ☑ ☐ ☐

revised once – some questions right ☑ ☑ ☐

revised twice – all questions right ☑ ☑ ☑

Move on to another topic when you have all three ticks

Distance–time graphs ☐ ☐ ☐

Velocity and acceleration ☐ ☐ ☐

More about velocity–time graphs ☐ ☐ ☐

Using graphs ☐ ☐ ☐

2.1 Forces between objects

Student Book
pages 176–177

P2

Key points

- A force can change the shape of an object or change its motion or state of rest.
- The unit of force is the newton (N).
- When two objects interact they always exert equal and opposite forces on each other.

Force of tyre on road   Force of road on tyre

Driving force

Key words: force, newton

- **Forces** are measured in **newtons**, abbreviated to N.
- Objects always exert **equal** and **opposite** forces on each other. If object A exerts a force on object B, object B exerts an equal and opposite force on object A. These are sometimes called 'action and reaction' forces.

> **1** *What is the SI unit of force?*

- If a car hits a barrier, it exerts a force on the barrier. The barrier exerts a force on the car that is equal in size and in the opposite direction.
- If you place a book on a table, the weight of the book will act vertically downwards on the table. The table will exert an equal and opposite reaction force upwards on the book.
- When a car is being driven forwards there is a force from the tyre on the ground pushing backwards. There is an equal and opposite force from the ground on the tyre which pushes the car forwards.

> **2** *In what direction does the force of weight always act?*

AQA *Examiner's tip*

> It is important to understand that action and reaction forces act on different objects. Remember that forces have both size and direction.

2.2 Resultant force

Student Book
pages 178–179

P2

Key points

- The resultant force is a single force that has the same effect as all the forces acting on an object.
- If an object is accelerating there must be a resultant force acting on it.

Bump up your grade

> If an object is accelerating it can be speeding up, slowing down or changing direction.

Key word: resultant force

- Most objects have more than one force acting on them. The **resultant force** is the single force that would have the same effect on the object as all the original forces acting together.
- When the resultant force on an object is zero:
  - if the object is at rest, it will stay at rest
  - if the object is moving, it will carry on moving at the same speed and in the same direction.

> **1** *What is the unit of resultant force?*

- When the resultant force on an object is not zero, there will be an acceleration in the direction of the force.
- This means that:
  - If the object is at rest, it will accelerate in the direction of the resultant force.
  - If the object is moving in the same direction as the resultant force, it will accelerate in that direction.
  - If the object is moving in the opposite direction to the resultant force, it will decelerate.

> **2** *What is the resultant force of a 4 N force and a 3 N force acting in the same direction?*

Student Book
pages 180–181 **P2**

2.3 Force and acceleration

- A **resultant force** always causes an **acceleration**. Remember that a deceleration is a negative acceleration. If there is no acceleration in a particular situation, the resultant force must be zero.

- Acceleration is a change in velocity. An object can accelerate by changing its direction even if it is going at a constant speed. So a resultant force is needed to make an object change direction.

- We can find the resultant force on an object using the equation:

$$F = m \times a$$

Where:
F is the resultant force in newtons, N
m is the mass in kilograms, kg
a is the acceleration in m/s².

- The greater the resultant force on an object, the greater its acceleration. The bigger the **mass** of an object, the bigger the force needed to give it a particular acceleration.

Key points

- The bigger the resultant force on an object, the greater its acceleration.

- The greater the mass of an object, the smaller its acceleration for a given force.

- $F = m \times a$

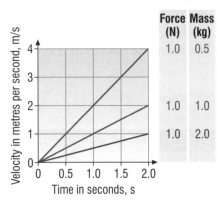

	Force (N)	Mass (kg)
	1.0	0.5
	1.0	1.0
	1.0	2.0

Velocity–time graph for different combinations of force and mass

▶ **1** *What happens to the acceleration of an object as the resultant force on it decreases?*

▶ **2** *What is the resultant force on a car of mass 1000 kg if its acceleration is 2 m/s²?*

Key word: mass

Student Book
pages 182–183 **P2**

2.4 On the road

- If a vehicle is travelling at a steady speed, the resultant force on it is zero. The driving forces are equal and opposite to the frictional forces.

▶ **1** *What is the resultant force on a car travelling at a steady speed on a straight horizontal road?*

- The faster the speed of a vehicle, the bigger the deceleration needed to stop it in a particular distance. So the bigger the braking force needed.

- The **stopping distance** of a vehicle is the distance it travels during the driver's reaction time (the thinking distance) plus the distance it travels under the braking force (the braking distance).

- The **thinking distance** is increased if the driver is tired or under the influence of alcohol or drugs.

- The **braking distance** can be increased by:
  - poorly maintained roads or bad weather conditions
  - the condition of the car. For example, worn tyres or worn brakes will increase braking distance.

▶ **2** *What is the relationship between stopping distance, thinking distance and braking distance?*

Key points

- Friction and air resistance oppose the driving force of a car.

- The stopping distance of a car depends on the thinking distance and the braking distance.

Bump up your grade

Remember that the reaction time depends on the driver. The braking distance depends on the road, weather conditions and the condition of the vehicle.

Key words: stopping distance, thinking distance, braking distance

2.5 Falling objects

- If an object falls freely, the resultant force acting on it is the force of gravity. It will make an object close to the Earth's surface accelerate at about 10 m/s².

- We call the force of gravity **weight**, and the acceleration the **acceleration due to gravity**.

- The equation:

$$F = m \times a$$

Where:
F is the resultant force in newtons, N
m is the mass in kilograms, kg
a is the acceleration in m/s²
becomes:

$$W = m \times g$$

Where:
W is the weight in newtons, N
m is the mass in kilograms, kg
g is the acceleration due to gravity in m/s².

- If the object is on the Earth, not falling, g is called the **gravitational field strength** and its units are newtons per kilogram, N/kg.

- When an object falls through a fluid, the fluid exerts a **drag force** on the object, resisting its motion. The faster the object falls, the bigger the drag force becomes, until eventually it will be equal to the weight of the object. The resultant force is now zero, so the body stops accelerating. It moves at a constant velocity called the **terminal velocity**.

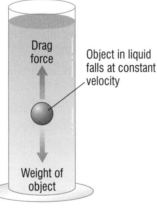

Drag force

Object in liquid falls at constant velocity

Weight of object

Falling in a liquid

➤ 1 *Why does an object dropped in a fluid initially accelerate?*
➤ 2 *What eventually happens to an object falling in a fluid?*

Key words: weight, gravitational field strength, drag force, terminal velocity

Student Book
pages 186–187 **P2**

2.6 Stretching and squashing

- If we hang small weights from a spring it will stretch. The increase in length from the original is called the **extension**. When we remove the weights the spring will return to its original length.
- Objects and materials that behave in this way are called **elastic**.
- An elastic object is one that regains its original shape when the forces deforming it are removed.

▮▮▮▶ **1** *What is an inelastic object?*

- If we plot a graph of extension against force applied for a spring, we obtain a straight line that passes though the origin. This tells us that the extension is **directly proportional** to the force applied. If we apply too big a force, the line begins to curve because we have exceeded the **limit of proportionality**.

Hooke's law

- Objects and materials that behave like this are said to obey **Hooke's law**. This states that the extension is directly proportional to the force applied, provided the limit of proportionality is not exceeded.
- We can write Hooke's law as an equation:

$$F = k \times e$$

Where:
F is the force applied in newtons, N
k is the **spring constant** of the spring in newtons per metre, N/m
e is the extension in metres, m.

- The stiffer a spring is, the greater its spring constant.
- When an elastic object is stretched, work is done. This is stored as elastic potential energy in the object.
- When the stretching force is removed, this stored energy is released.

▮▮▮▶ **2** *A spring has a spring constant of 30 N/m. If the extension is 0.30 m, what is the force applied?*

▮▮▮▶ **3** *How can we tell when a spring has exceeded its limit of proportionality?*

Key words: elastic, directly proportional, limit of proportionality, Hooke's law

Key points

- The extension is the difference between the length of the spring and its original length.
- The extension of a spring is directly proportional to the force applied to it, provided the limit of proportionality is not exceeded.
- The spring constant of a spring is the force per unit extension needed to stretch it.

AQA Examiner's tip

Two quantities are directly proportional to each other only if plotting them on a graph gives a straight line through the origin.

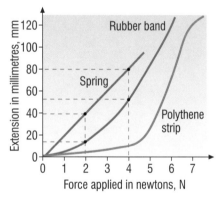

Extension versus force applied for different materials

Student Book
pages 188–189

P2

2.7 Force and speed issues

- Fuel economy of road vehicles can be improved by reducing the speed or fitting a wind deflector.

- Average speed cameras are linked in pairs and they measure the average speed of a vehicle.

- Anti-skid surfaces increase the friction between a car tyre and the road surface. This reduces skids, or even prevents skids altogether.

- Reducing the speed of a vehicle reduces the amount of fuel it uses to travel a particular distance. This is called fuel economy.

- Reducing the air resistance by making the vehicle more streamlined (e.g. fitting a wind deflector) also improves fuel economy.

- Speed cameras are used to discourage motorists from speeding. They can determine the speed of a motorist at a particular point. They can also be used in pairs to determine the speed at two points and so calculate an average speed. Motorists caught travelling above the speed limit are fined and may lose their driving licence.

- Skidding happens when the brakes on a vehicle are applied too harshly. When a vehicle skids the wheels lock and slide along the road surface, increasing the stopping distance.

- Anti-skid surfaces are used to reduce or prevent skidding. They are rougher than normal road surfaces, increasing the friction between the vehicle tyres and the road. They are used in places where drivers are likely to brake, such as near traffic lights and road junctions.

1 *Why does making a vehicle more streamlined improve fuel economy?*

2 *When a vehicle is travelling along a straight road at a steady speed what can you say about the engine force and the air resistance?*

A speed camera

1 If you push on a wall with a horizontal force of 15 N to the right, what force will the wall exert on you?

2 What happens to an object moving at a steady speed if the resultant force on it is zero?

3 When will a resultant force cause a deceleration?

4 What happens to the acceleration of an object as the resultant force on it increases?

5 What is the resultant force on a car of mass 1500 kg if its acceleration is 0.5 m/s²?

6 What is the acceleration of a car of mass 2000 kg if the resultant force acting in its direction of motion is 800 N?

7 What is the effect of the speed of a vehicle on its stopping distance?

8 What is terminal velocity?

9 What is the weight of a person of mass 70 kg?

10 What is an elastic object?

11 What does Hooke's law state?

12 When a force of 10 N is applied to a spring it extends by 2.0 cm. What is the spring constant of the spring?

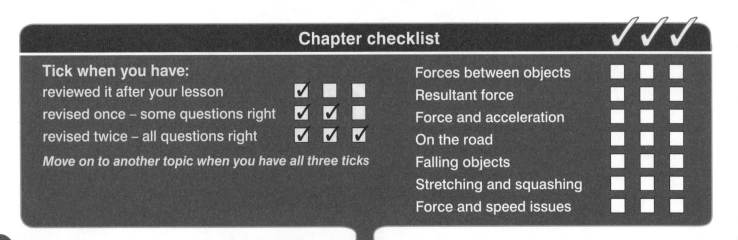

Chapter checklist

Tick when you have:
reviewed it after your lesson ☑ ☐ ☐
revised once – some questions right ☑ ☑ ☐
revised twice – all questions right ☑ ☑ ☑
Move on to another topic when you have all three ticks

Forces between objects ☐ ☐ ☐
Resultant force ☐ ☐ ☐
Force and acceleration ☐ ☐ ☐
On the road ☐ ☐ ☐
Falling objects ☐ ☐ ☐
Stretching and squashing ☐ ☐ ☐
Force and speed issues ☐ ☐ ☐

Student Book
pages 192–193

P2

3.1 Energy and work

Key points

- Work is done on an object when a force makes the object move.
- Energy transferred = work done
- $W = F \times d$
- Work done to overcome friction is transferred as energy that heats the objects that rub together and the surroundings.

Key words: work, friction

- Whenever an object starts to move, a force must have been applied to it.
- When a force moves an object, energy is transferred and **work** is done.
- When work is done moving the object, the supplied energy is transferred to the object so the work done is equal to the energy transferred.
- Both work and energy have the unit joule, J.
- The work done on an object is calculated using the equation:

$$W = F \times d$$

Where:
W is the work done in joules, J
F is the force in newtons, N
d is the distance moved in the direction of the force in metres, m.
Note that if the distance moved is zero, no work is done on the object.

- Work done to overcome **friction** is mainly transferred into energy by heating. When the brakes are applied to a vehicle, friction between the brake pads and the wheel discs opposes the motion of the wheel. The kinetic energy of the vehicle is transferred into energy that heats the brake pads and the wheel discs as well as the surrounding air.

> **1** *What is the SI unit of work done?*
> **2** *What is the work done on an object if a force of 300 N moves it a distance of 8 m?*

Student Book
pages 194–195

P2

3.2 Gravitational potential energy

Key points

- The gravitational potential energy of an object depends on its weight and how far it moves vertically.
- $E_p = m \times g \times h$

AQA Examiner's tip

Remember that the gravitational potential energy an object has is relative to another point, usually to the surface of the Earth. So we calculate changes in gravitational potential energy when an object is moved between two points.

Key words: gravitational potential energy, power

- **Gravitational potential energy** is energy stored in an object because of its position in the Earth's gravitational field. Whenever an object is moved vertically upwards it gains gravitational potential energy equal to the work done on it by the lifting force.
- The change in gravitational potential energy can be calculated using the equation:

$$E_p = m \times g \times h$$

Where:
E_p is the change in gravitational potential energy in joules, J
m is the mass in kilograms, kg
g is the gravitational field strength in newtons per kilogram, N/kg
h is the change in height in metres, m.

> **1** *What is the increase in E_p when a mass of 40 kg is lifted 8 m vertically?*

- **Power** is the rate of transfer of energy. Power can be calculated using the equation:

$$P = \frac{E}{t}$$

Where:
P is the power in watts, W
E is the energy in joules, J
t is the time in seconds, s.

> **2** *It takes 2 seconds to lift the object in Question 1. What is the power developed?*

Student Book
pages 196–197

P2

3.3 Kinetic energy

Student Book
pages 196–197

Key points

- The kinetic energy of a moving object depends on its mass and its speed.
- $E_k = \frac{1}{2} \times m \times v^2$
- Elastic potential energy is the energy stored in an elastic object when work is done on the object.

Bump up your grade

If an elastic band is stretched and released, elastic potential energy is transferred to kinetic energy.

- All moving objects have **kinetic energy.** The greater the mass and the faster the speed of an object, the more kinetic energy it has.
- Kinetic energy can be calculated using the equation:

$$E_k = \frac{1}{2} \times m \times v^2$$

Where:
E_k is the kinetic energy in joules, J
m is the mass in kilograms, kg
v is the speed in metres per second, m/s.

> **1** *A boy of mass 40 kg runs at a speed of 5 m/s. What is his kinetic energy?*

- An object is described as being **elastic** if it regains its shape after being stretched or squashed. When work is done on an elastic object to stretch or squash it, the energy transferred to it is stored as **elastic potential energy**. When the object returns to its original shape, this energy is released.

> **2** *When a spring is squashed and released it warms up. Why?*

Key words: kinetic energy, elastic potential energy

Student Book
pages 198–199

P2

3.4 Momentum

Key points

- $p = m \times v$
- The unit of momentum is kg m/s.
- Momentum is conserved whenever objects interact, provided no external forces act on them.

AQA Examiner's tip

Remember that momentum has a size and a direction.

Bump up your grade

The unit of momentum is kg m/s, or you may see this written as Ns.

- All moving objects have **momentum**. The greater the mass and the greater the velocity of an object, the greater its momentum.

> **1** *When do objects have momentum?*

- Momentum can be calculated using the equation:

$$p = m \times v$$

Where:
p is the momentum in kilogram metres per second, kg m/s
m is the mass in kilograms, kg
v is the velocity in metres per second, m/s.

> **2** *What is the momentum of a 1000 kg car travelling at 30 m/s?*

- Whenever objects interact, the total momentum before the interaction is equal to the total momentum afterwards – provided no external forces act on them.
- This is called the law of **conservation of momentum.**
- Another way to say this is that the total change in momentum is zero.
- The interaction could be a collision or an explosion. After a collision the objects may move off together, or they may move apart.

Key words: momentum, conservation of momentum

Student Book
pages 200–201

P2

3.5 Explosions

Key points

- Momentum = mass × velocity; and velocity is speed in a certain direction.
- When two objects push each other apart, they move apart:
  - with different speeds if they have unequal masses
  - with equal and opposite momentum so their total momentum is zero.

An artillery gun in action

- Like velocity, momentum has both size and direction.
- In calculations, one direction must be defined as positive, so momentum in the opposite direction is negative.
- When two objects are at rest their momentum is zero. In an explosion the objects move apart with equal and opposite momentum. One momentum is positive and the other negative, so the total momentum after the explosion is zero.
- Firing a bullet from a gun is an example of an explosion. The bullet moves off with a momentum in one direction and the gun 'recoils' with equal momentum in the opposite direction.

▹ **1** *What is the total momentum after an explosion equal to?*

▹ **2** *Two students on roller skates stand holding each other in the playground. They push each other away. What can you say about the momentum of each student?*

AQA *Examiner's tip*

In calculations involving the conservation of momentum and collisions or explosions, it often helps if you sketch a diagram to show where the objects are before and after the collision or explosion.

Student Book
pages 202–203

P2

3.6 Impact forces

Key points

- When vehicles collide, the force of the impact depends on mass, change of velocity and the duration of the impact.
- When two vehicles collide:
  - they exert equal and opposite forces on each other
  - their total momentum is unchanged.

Bump up your grade

Make sure that you can explain how crumple zones in cars reduce the forces acting by increasing the time taken to change the momentum of a car.

- When a force acts on an object that is able to move, or is moving, its momentum changes.
- For a particular change in momentum the longer the time taken for the change, the smaller the force that acts.
- In a collision, the momentum of an object often becomes zero during the impact – the object comes to rest.
- If the **impact time** is short, the forces on the object are large. As the impact time increases, the forces become less.

▹ **1** *What is impact time?*

Crumple zones in cars are designed to fold in a collision. This increases the impact time and so reduces the force on the car and the people in it.

▹ **2** *Why do cars have crumple zones at both the front and the rear?*

Key words: impact time, crumple zone

3.7 Car safety ⚙

Key points

- Seat belts and air bags spread the force across the chest and they also increase the impact time.

- Side impact bars and crumple zones 'give way' in an impact so increasing the impact time.

- We can use the conservation of momentum to find the speed of a car before an impact.

An airbag in action

- Modern cars contain a number of safety features designed to reduce the forces on the occupants of the car in a collision.

- Side impact bars and crumple zones fold up in a collision to increase the impact time and reduce the forces acting.

- **Seat belts** and **air bags** spread the forces on the body across a larger area. If a driver's head hits an airbag it changes momentum slowly, so the force on the head is less than it would be if it changed momentum quickly by hitting the steering wheel.

- A seat belt stops the wearer being flung forward if the car stops suddenly. The seatbelt stretches slightly increasing the impact time and reducing the force.

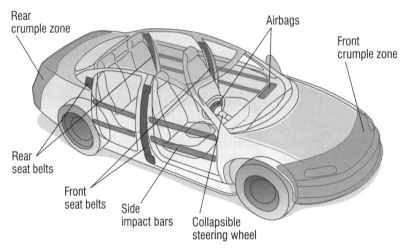

Rear crumple zone
Airbags
Front crumple zone
Rear seat belts
Front seat belts
Side impact bars
Collapsible steering wheel

Car safety features

▶ **1** *What happens to a passenger in a head-on collision:*
   a *if they are not wearing a seat belt?*
   b *if they were wearing a very narrow seat belt?*

After a car crash the police use measurements from the scene and the conservation of momentum to calculate the speed of the vehicles before the collision.

AQA *Examiner's tip*

Make sure that you can explain how different vehicle safety features work in terms of spreading out and reducing the forces on the occupants of the vehicle.

1 When is work done by a force?

2 What is the relationship between work and energy?

3 What is the unit of power?

4 What is the decrease in gravitational potential energy when an object of mass 6 kg is lowered through a distance of 9 m?

5 What is elastic potential energy?

6 What is the kinetic energy of a car of mass 1200 kg travelling at 30 m/s?

7 What is the unit of momentum?

8 What is the momentum of a 2500 kg truck travelling at 20 m/s?

9 Why is a gymnast less likely to injure herself if she lands on a thick foam mat than if she lands on a hard floor?

10 An electric motor is used to raise a 0.1 kg mass vertically upwards. If the mass gains 2 J of gravitational potential energy, calculate the height it is raised through. [H]

11 The electronic motor in Question 10 has a power of 1.5 W. Calculate the time taken to raise the load. [H]

12 A trolley of mass 0.2 kg travelling at 1.5 m/s to the right collides with a stationary trolley of mass 0.3 kg. After the collision they move off together. Calculate the velocity of the trolleys after the collision. [H]

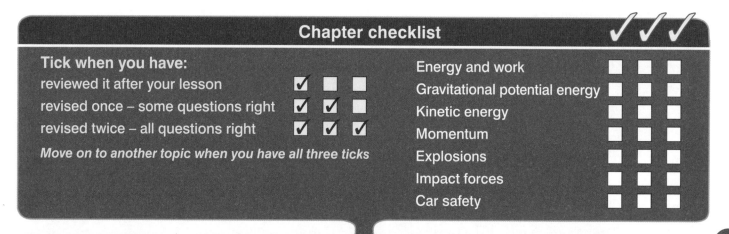

Chapter checklist			✓	✓	✓
Tick when you have:					
reviewed it after your lesson	✓	▢	▢	Energy and work	▢ ▢ ▢
revised once – some questions right	✓	✓	▢	Gravitational potential energy	▢ ▢ ▢
revised twice – all questions right	✓	✓	✓	Kinetic energy	▢ ▢ ▢
Move on to another topic when you have all three ticks				Momentum	▢ ▢ ▢
				Explosions	▢ ▢ ▢
				Impact forces	▢ ▢ ▢
				Car safety	▢ ▢ ▢

Student Book
pages 208–209 **P2**

4.1 Electrical charges

Key points

- Certain insulating materials become charged when rubbed together.
- Electrons are transferred when objects become charged.
- Like charges repel; unlike charges attract.

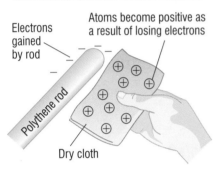

Electrons gained by rod

Atoms become positive as a result of losing electrons

Polythene rod

Dry cloth

Charging by friction

- When two electrically **insulating** materials are rubbed together, **electrons** are rubbed off one material and deposited on the other. Which way the electrons are transferred depends on the particular materials.
- Electrons have a **negative** charge so the material that has gained electrons becomes negatively charged. The one that has lost electrons is left with a **positive** charge. This process is called charging by friction.

▶ **1** *How does an insulator become negatively charged?*

- Two objects that have opposite electric charges **attract** each other. Two objects that have the same electric charges **repel** each other.
- The bigger the distance between the objects, the weaker the force between them.

▶ **2** *What will happen if two negatively charged objects are brought close together?*

Key words: insulating, electron, attract, repel

Student Book
pages 210–211 **P2**

4.2 Electric circuits

Key points

- Every component has its own agreed symbol.
- $I = \dfrac{Q}{t}$

AQA *Examiner's tip*

Make sure that you can recognise and draw all of these circuit symbols. Use a sharp pencil and make sure there are no gaps or odd ends of wire shown on your diagram.

- Every component in a circuit has an agreed **circuit symbol**. These are put together in a circuit diagram to show how the components are connected together in a circuit.

$$I = \frac{Q}{t}$$

Where:
I is the current in amperes, A
Q is the charge in coulombs, C
t is the time in seconds, s.

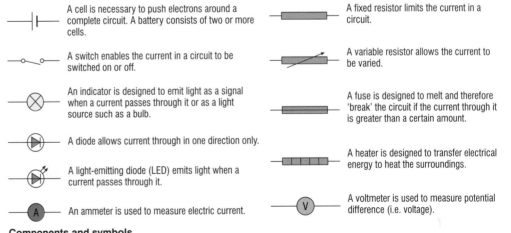

A cell is necessary to push electrons around a complete circuit. A battery consists of two or more cells.

A switch enables the current in a circuit to be switched on or off.

An indicator is designed to emit light as a signal when a current passes through it or as a light source such as a bulb.

A diode allows current through in one direction only.

A light-emitting diode (LED) emits light when a current passes through it.

An ammeter is used to measure electric current.

A fixed resistor limits the current in a circuit.

A variable resistor allows the current to be varied.

A fuse is designed to melt and therefore 'break' the circuit if the current through it is greater than a certain amount.

A heater is designed to transfer electrical energy to heat the surroundings.

A voltmeter is used to measure potential difference (i.e. voltage).

Components and symbols

▶ **1** *What is the circuit symbol for a closed switch?*
▶ **2** *What is the circuit symbol for a battery of three cells?*

Student Book
pages 212–213 **P2**

4.3 Resistance

Key points

- $V = \dfrac{W}{Q} = \dfrac{E}{Q}$

- $R = \dfrac{V}{I}$

- Ohm's law states that the current through a resistor at constant temperature is directly proportional to the potential difference across the resistor.

- Reversing the current through a component reverses the potential difference across it.

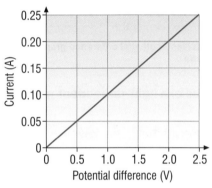

A current–potential difference graph for a resistor

AQA **Examiner's tip**

Ammeters are always connected in series and voltmeters are always connected in parallel.

- The current through a component is measured with an ammeter. Ammeters are always placed in **series** with the component. The unit of current is the ampere (or amp), A.

- The **potential difference** (pd), across a component is measured with a voltmeter. Voltmeters are always placed in **parallel** with the component. The unit of potential difference is the **volt, V**.

▐▶ **1** *What device is used to measure current?*

- Potential difference, work done and charge are related by the equation:

$$V = \frac{W}{Q}$$

Where:
V is the potential difference in volts, V
W is the work done in joules, J
Q is the charge in coulombs, C.

- As work done is equal to energy transferred we can also say that:

$$V = \frac{E}{Q}$$

Where:
E is the energy transferred in joules, J.

- **Resistance** is the opposition to current flow. The unit of resistance is the ohm, Ω.

- The resistance of a component is calculated using the equation:

$$R = \frac{V}{I}$$

Where:
R is resistance in ohms, Ω
V is potential difference in volts, V
I is current in amps, A.

- Current–potential difference graphs are used to show how the current through a component varies with the potential difference across it.

Ohm's law

- If a resistor is kept at a constant temperature, the current–potential difference graph shows a straight line passing through the origin. This means the current is directly proportional to the potential difference (pd) across the resistor. This is known as **Ohm's law**. Any component that obeys Ohm's law is called an **ohmic conductor**.

▐▶ **2** *What is the unit of resistance?*

Key words: series, potential difference, parallel, volt (V), resistance, Ohm's law, ohmic conductor

Student Book
pages 214–215 **P2**

4.4 More current–potential difference graphs

Key points

- *Filament bulb:* resistance increases with increase of the filament temperature.
- *Diode:* 'forward' resistance low; 'reverse' resistance high.
- *Thermistor:* resistance decreases if its temperature increases.
- *LDR:* resistance decreases if the light intensity on it increases.

AQA *Examiner's tip*

Current–potential difference may be plotted with the current on the *x*-axis or the *y*-axis. Make sure you know the shape either way round and check which way round they are given in exam questions.

- The line on a current–potential difference graph for a **filament bulb** is a curve. So the current is not directly proportional to the potential difference.
- The resistance of the filament increases as the current increases. This is because the resistance increases as the temperature increases.
- Reversing the potential difference makes no difference to the shape of the curve.
- The current through a **diode** flows in one direction only. In the reverse direction the diode has a very high resistance so the current is zero.

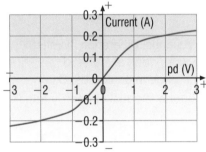

A current–potential difference graph for a filament bulb

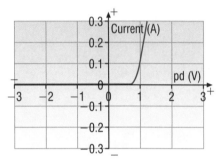

A current–potential difference graph for a diode

- As the light falling on it gets brighter, the resistance of a **light-dependent resistor** (LDR) decreases.
- As the temperature goes up, the resistance of a **thermistor** goes down.

> 1 *What happens to the resistance of an LDR if its surroundings become darker?*
> 2 *What effect does reversing the pd across a filament bulb have on the current–potential difference curve?*

Key words: filament bulb, diode, light-dependent resistor, thermistor

Student Book
pages 216–217 **P2**

4.5 Series circuits

Key points

- For components in series:
  - the current is the same in each component
  - adding the potential differences gives the total potential difference
  - adding the resistances gives the total resistance.

- In a **series** circuit the components are connected one after another. Therefore if there is a break anywhere in the circuit, charge stops flowing.
- There is no choice of route for the charge as it flows around the circuit, so the current through each component is the same.

> 1 *What happens in a series circuit if one component stops working?*

- The current depends on the potential difference (pd) of the **supply** and the total resistance of the circuit:

$$I = \frac{V}{R}$$

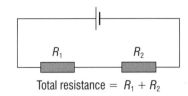

Total resistance = $R_1 + R_2$

Resistors in series

- The pd of the supply is shared between all the components in the circuit. So the pds across individual components add up to give the pd of the supply.
- The resistances of the individual components in series add up to give the total resistance of the circuit.
- The bigger the resistance of a component, the bigger its share of the supply pd.

▐▐▐▶ **2** *How could you find the total resistance in a series circuit?*

Student Book
pages 218–219

P2

4.6 Parallel circuits

Key points

- For components in parallel:
  - the total current is the sum of the currents through the separate components
  - the bigger the resistance of a component the smaller the current is.
- In a parallel circuit the potential difference is the same across each component.
- To calculate the current through a resistor in a parallel circuit use $I = \dfrac{V}{R}$

▲ Bump up your grade

In everyday life, parallel circuits are much more useful than series circuits. That is because a break in one part of the circuit does not stop charge flowing in the rest of the circuit.

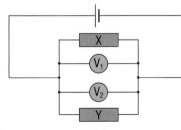

Components in parallel

- In a **parallel** circuit each component is connected across the supply, so if there is a break in one part of the circuit, charge can still flow in the other parts.
- Each component is connected across the supply pd, so the pd across each component is the same.
- There are junctions in the circuit so different amounts of charge can flow through different components. The current through each component depends on its resistance. The bigger the resistance of a component, the smaller the current through it.

▐▐▐▶ **1** *What happens in a parallel circuit if one component stops working?*

- The current through a component in a parallel circuit can be calculated using
$$I = \frac{V}{R}$$
- The total current through the whole circuit is equal to the sum of the currents through the separate components.

▐▐▐▶ **2** *In a parallel circuit what is the relationship between the supply pd and the pd across each parallel component?*

🖩 Maths skills

Two $4\,\Omega$ resistors are connected in parallel across a $12\,V$ battery. Calculate the total current through the battery.

pd across each resistor = pd across the battery

For each resistor $V = I \times R$
$$I = \frac{V}{R}$$
$$I = \frac{12\,V}{4\,\Omega}$$
$$I = 3\,A$$

Total current = $3\,A + 3\,A = 6\,A$

AQA Examiner's tip

Make sure that you understand the difference between series and parallel circuits.

1 What sort of charge does an electron have?

2 In terms of electrons, how does an insulator become positively charged?

3 What sort of force will there be between two negatively charged objects?

4 Draw a circuit diagram for a circuit containing a cell, a bulb, a resistor and a switch, connected one after the other.

5 If the current through a component is 0.2 A when the potential difference across it is 12 V, what is its resistance?

6 The energy transferred to a bulb is 36 J when 8.0 C of charge passes through it. Calculate the potential difference across the bulb.

7 What is an ohmic conductor?

8 Explain the shape of the line on a current–potential difference graph for a diode.

9 A series circuit contains a variable resistor. If its resistance is increased, what happens to the pd across it?

10 A 5 Ω resistor and an 8 Ω resistor are connected in series. What is their total resistance?

11 Where should an ammeter and a voltmeter be placed in a circuit to measure the current through, and the pd across, a resistor?

12 A 4 Ω resistor and a 12 Ω resistor are connected in series with a 12 V battery. What is the current in the circuit?

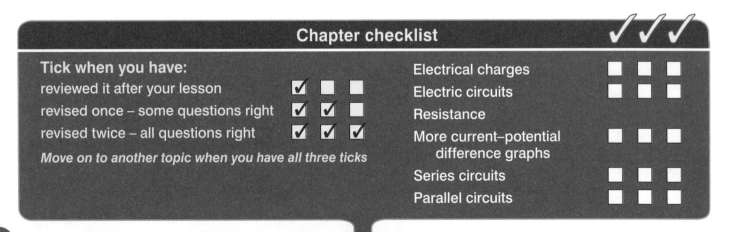

Chapter checklist			✓ ✓ ✓
Tick when you have:			Electrical charges
reviewed it after your lesson	✓ ☐ ☐		Electric circuits
revised once – some questions right	✓ ✓ ☐		Resistance
revised twice – all questions right	✓ ✓ ✓		More current–potential difference graphs
Move on to another topic when you have all three ticks			Series circuits
			Parallel circuits

5.1 Alternating current

- Cells and batteries supply current that passes round the circuit in one direction.
- This is called **direct current**, or dc.
- The current from the mains supply passes in one direction, then reverses and passes in the other direction.
- This is called **alternating current**, or ac.

▶ **1** *What is direct current?*

- The **frequency** of the UK mains supply is 50 hertz (Hz), which means it changes direction 50 times each second. The 'voltage' of the mains is 230 V.
- The **live wire** of the mains supply alternates between a positive and a negative potential with respect to the **neutral wire**. The neutral wire stays at zero volts.
- The live wire alternates between **peak voltages** of +325 V and −325 V. In terms of electrical power, this is equivalent to a direct potential difference of 230 V.

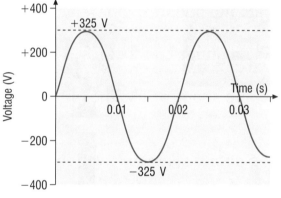

Graph of mains voltage against time

▶ **2** *What is the potential of the neutral terminal?*

The frequency of an ac supply can be determined from an **oscilloscope** trace using the equation

$$f = \frac{1}{T}$$

Where:
f is the frequency of the ac in hertz, Hz
T is the time for one cycle in seconds, s.

Key words: direct current, alternating current, frequency, live wire, neutral wire, oscilloscope

Key points

- Direct current is in one direction only. Alternating current repeatedly reverses its direction.

- The peak voltage of an alternating potential difference is the maximum voltage measured from zero volts.

- A mains circuit has a live wire that is alternately positive and negative every cycle and a neutral wire at zero volts.

$f = \frac{1}{T}$ [H]

Bump up your grade

Make sure that you can make readings from diagrams of oscilloscope traces.

Higher

5.2 Cables and plugs

Key points

- Sockets and plugs are made of stiff plastic materials, which enclose the electrical connections.

- Cables consist of two or three insulated copper wires surrounded by an outer layer of flexible plastic material.

- In a three-pin plug or a three-core cable:
  - the live wire is brown
  - the neutral wire is blue
  - the earth wire is green and yellow.

- The earth wire is used to earth the metal case of a mains appliance.

Mains cable

- Most electrical appliances are connected to the **sockets** of the mains supply using **cable** and a **three-pin plug**.

- The outer cover of a three-pin plug is made of plastic or rubber. Both these materials are good electrical insulators.

- The pins of the plug are made of brass. Brass is a good electrical conductor. It is also hard and will not rust or oxidise.

- The earth wire is connected to the longest pin.

- It is important that the cable grip is fastened tightly over the cable. There should be no bare wires showing inside the plug and the correct cable must be connected firmly to the terminal of the correct pin.

- The brown wire is connected to the live pin.

- The blue wire is connected to the neutral pin.

- The green and yellow wire (of a three-core cable) is connected to the earth pin. A two-core cable does not have an earth wire.

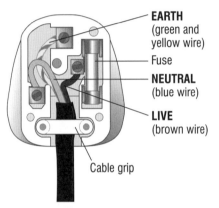

EARTH (green and yellow wire)
Fuse
NEUTRAL (blue wire)
LIVE (brown wire)
Cable grip

Inside a three-pin plug

 1 *Why are the pins of a plug made of brass?*

- Appliances with metal cases must be earthed – the case is attached to the earth wire in the cable.

- Appliances with plastic cases do not need to be earthed. They are said to be double insulated and are connected to the supply with two-core cable containing just a live and a neutral wire.

2 *Why must appliances with metal cases be earthed?*

- Cables of different thicknesses are used for different purposes. The more current to be carried, the thicker the cable needs to be.

AQA *Examiner's tip*

Make sure that you can identify faults in the wiring of a three-pin plug.

Key words: socket, cable, three-pin plug

5.3 Fuses

- A fuse contains a thin wire that heats up and melts if too much current passes through it. This cuts off the current.

- A circuit breaker is an electromagnetic switch that opens (i.e. 'trips') and cuts the current off if too much current passes through it.

Bump up your grade

Make sure you can explain how the earth wire and the fuse wire work together to protect an appliance.

- A mains appliance with a plastic case does not need to be earthed because plastic is an insulator and cannot become live.

- Appliances with metal cases need to be earthed. Otherwise if a fault develops, and the live wire touches the metal case, the case becomes live and could give a shock to anyone who touches it.

- A **fuse** is always fitted in series with the live wire. This cuts the appliance off from the live wire if the fuse blows.

- If a fault develops in an earthed appliance, a large current flows to earth and melts the fuse, disconnecting the supply.

- The rating of the fuse should be slightly higher than the normal working current of the appliance. If it is much higher, it will not melt soon enough. If it is not higher than the normal current, it will melt as soon as the appliance is switched on.

▷ **1** *What is a fuse?*

- A **circuit breaker** can be used in place of a fuse. This is an electromagnetic switch that opens and cuts off the supply if the current is bigger than a certain value.

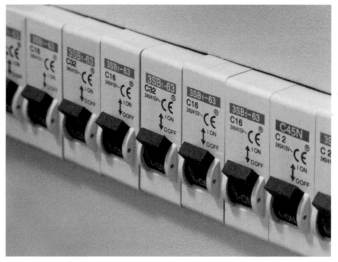

A circuit breaker

- A **residual current circuit breaker (RCCB)** cuts off the current in the live wire if it is different to the current in the neutral wire. It works faster than a fuse or an ordinary circuit breaker.

▷ **2** *Why don't appliances with plastic cases need to be earthed?*

Key words: fuse, circuit breaker, residual current circuit breaker (RCCB)

5.4 Electrical power and potential difference

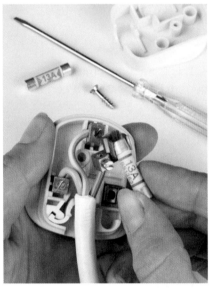

Changing a fuse

- An electrical appliance transfers electrical energy into other forms of energy.
- The rate at which it does this is called the power.
- Power can be calculated using the equation:

$$P = \frac{E}{t}$$

Where:
P is the power in watts, W
E is the energy transferred in joules, J
t is the time in seconds, s.

⟫ 1 *What is the power, in kW, of an appliance that transfers 90 000 J of energy in 30 seconds?*

In an electric circuit it is more usual to measure the current through an appliance and the potential difference across it rather than the energy transferred and the time.

We can also use current and pd to calculate the power of the appliance using the equation:

$$P = I \times V$$

Where:
P is the power in watts, W
I is the current in amperes, A
V is the potential difference in volts, V.

- Electrical appliances have their power rating shown on them. The pd of the mains supply is 230 V.

- This equation can be used to calculate the normal current through an appliance and so work out the size of fuse to use.

- The fuse is chosen so that its value is slightly higher than the calculated current.

Maths skills

What is the current in a steam wallpaper stripper that has a power of 2 kW?

$P = I \times V$

$I = \dfrac{P}{V}$

$I = 2000\,\text{W}/230\,\text{V}$

$I = 8.7\,\text{A}$

⟫ 2 *What is the power of a mains appliance that takes a current of 10 A?*

Student Book
pages 230–231 **P2**

5.5 Electrical energy and charge

Key points

- An electric current is the rate of flow of charge.
- $Q = I \times t$
- When charge flows through a resistor, energy transferred to the resistor makes it hot.
- $E = V \times Q$ **[H]**

AQA Examiner's tip

When a charge flows in a circuit the components will heat up. This means that most electrical appliances have vents to keep them cool.

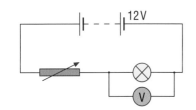

Energy transfer in a circuit

- An electric current is the rate of flow of **charge**.
- The equation relating charge, current and time is:

$$Q = I \times t$$

Where:
Q is the charge in coulombs, C
I is the current in amperes, A
t is the time in seconds, s.

➠ **1** *How much charge flows past a particular point in a circuit when a current of 2 A flows for 2 minutes?*

- When charge flows through an appliance, electrical energy is transferred to other forms. In a resistor, electrical energy is transferred to the resistor so the resistor becomes hotter.

Energy, potential difference and charge

The amount of energy transferred can be calculated using the equation:

$$E = V \times Q$$

Where:
E is the energy in joules, J
V is the potential difference in volts, V
Q is the charge in coulombs, C.

➠ **2** *How much energy is transferred when a charge of 200 C flows through a resistor that has a potential difference across it of 230 V?*

Higher

Student Book
pages 232–233 **P2**

5.6 Electrical issues ⚙️

Key points

- Electrical faults are dangerous because they can cause electric shocks and fires.
- Never touch a mains appliance (or plug or socket) with wet hands. Never touch a bare wire or a terminal at a potential of more than 30 V.
- Check cables, plugs and sockets for damage regularly.

AQA Examiner's tip

You may have to identify the best appliance to use in a particular situation from information given in a question.

- **Electrical faults** may occur as a result of damage to sockets, plugs, cables or appliances.
- Electrical equipment should be checked regularly for wear. Worn or damaged items should be replaced or repaired by a qualified electrician.
- Avoid overloading sockets, as this may cause overheating and a risk of fire.
- Electrical appliances should be handled safely and never used in a bathroom or with wet hands.
- The cable should always be appropriate for the intended use.

➠ **1** *Why can two-core cable be used for a hairdryer?*

- When choosing an electrical appliance, the power and efficiency rating need to be considered, as well as the cost.
- Filament bulbs and halogen bulbs are much less efficient than low-energy bulbs and do not last as long.
- There are a number of different low-energy bulbs available.

➠ **2** *Why are filament bulbs very inefficient?*

1 What is the potential difference of the mains supply?

2 What is the frequency of the mains supply?

3 What is the peak voltage of the mains supply?

4 What colour is the neutral wire?

5 What does the cover on an earth wire look like?

6 Why is the outer cover of a three-pin plug made of plastic?

7 What fuse should be used in a 500 W mains heater?

8 What is the unit of charge?

9 What is a circuit breaker?

10 How much energy is transferred when a 2 kW appliance is used for 15 seconds?

11 What is the current through a 2300 W mains heater?

12 24 000 J of energy are transferred when 2000 C of charge flow through a bulb. What is the potential difference across the bulb? [H]

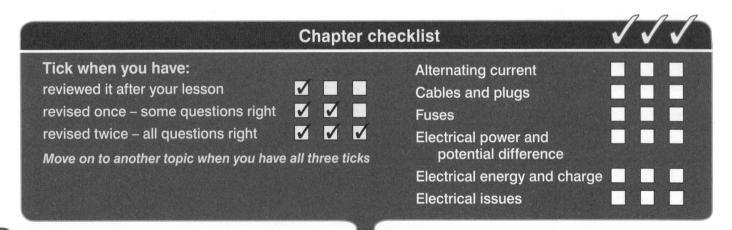

Chapter checklist

Tick when you have:
reviewed it after your lesson ✓ ☐ ☐
revised once – some questions right ✓ ✓ ☐
revised twice – all questions right ✓ ✓ ✓
Move on to another topic when you have all three ticks

Alternating current ☐ ☐ ☐
Cables and plugs ☐ ☐ ☐
Fuses ☐ ☐ ☐
Electrical power and potential difference ☐ ☐ ☐
Electrical energy and charge ☐ ☐ ☐
Electrical issues ☐ ☐ ☐

Student Book
pages 236–237

P2

6.1 Observing nuclear radiation

- The basic structure of an atom is a small central **nucleus**, made up of **protons** and **neutrons**, surrounded by **electrons**.

- The nuclei of radioactive substances are unstable. They become stable by **radioactive decay**. In this process, they emit radiation and turn into other elements.

- The three types of radiation emitted are: **alpha radiation**, **beta radiation**, **gamma radiation**.

▷ **1** *Which part of an atom might emit alpha particles?*

- We cannot predict when an unstable nucleus will decay. It is a random process and is not affected by external conditions.

- **Background radiation** is around us all the time. This is radiation from radioactive substances in the environment, from space, from devices such as X-ray tubes.

▷ **2** *What happens to the rate of radioactive decay if the temperature is doubled?*

Key words: nucleus, proton, neutron, electron, alpha radiation, beta radiation, gamma radiation

Student Book
pages 238–239

P2

6.2 The discovery of the nucleus

- At one time scientists thought that atoms consisted of spheres of positive charge with electrons stuck into them, like plums in a pudding. So this became known as the 'plum pudding' model of the atom.

- Then Rutherford, Geiger and Marsden devised an **alpha particle scattering** experiment, in which they fired alpha particles at thin gold foil.

- Most of the alpha particles passed straight through the foil. This means that most of the atom is just empty space.

- Some of the alpha particles were deflected through small angles. This suggests that the nucleus has a positive charge.

- A few rebound through very large angles. This suggests that the nucleus has a large mass and a very large positive charge.

▷ **1** *Why did most alpha particles pass straight through the foil in Rutherford's experiment?*

▷ **2** *What did the alpha particle scattering experiment suggest about the structure of the nucleus?*

Bump up your grade

The alpha particle has a positive charge. Because some of the alpha particles rebound, they must be repelled by another positive charge.

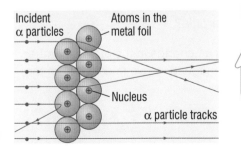

Incident α particles — Atoms in the metal foil

Nucleus

α particle tracks

Alpha particle scattering

6.3 Nuclear reactions

	Change in the nucleus	Particle emitted
α decay	The nucleus loses 2 protons and 2 neutrons	2 protons and 2 neutrons emitted as an α particle
β decay	A neutron in the nucleus changes into a proton and an electron	The electron created in the nucleus is instantly emitted

Key points

- Isotopes of an element are atoms with the same number of protons but different numbers of neutrons. Therefore they have the same atomic numbers but different mass numbers.

- The table below gives the relative masses and charges of these particles.

	Relative mass	Relative charge
Proton	1	+1
Neutron	1	0
Electron	0.0005	−1

Examiner's tip

Make sure you can use nuclear equations to show how the atomic number and mass number change when alpha or beta particles are emitted. **[H]**

- In an atom the number of protons = number of electrons, so the atom has no overall charge. If an atom loses or gains electrons it becomes charged and is called an **ion**.

- All atoms of a particular element have the same number of protons. Atoms of the same element with different numbers of neutrons are called **isotopes**.

- The number of protons in an atom is its **atomic number**.

- The total number of protons plus neutrons in an atom is its **mass number**.

- An alpha particle consists of two protons and two neutrons. It has a relative mass of 4 and its relative charge is +2. We represent it as $^4_2\alpha$.

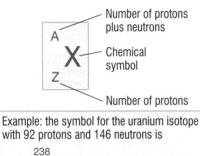

Number of protons plus neutrons

$^A_Z X$

Chemical symbol

Number of protons

Example: the symbol for the uranium isotope with 92 protons and 146 neutrons is

$^{238}_{92}U$ (or sometimes U-238)

Representing an isotope

When a nucleus emits an alpha particle the atomic number goes down by two and the mass number goes down by four.

For example, radium emits an alpha particle and becomes radon.

▶ **1** *What is the relative charge of an alpha particle?*

- A beta particle is a high-speed electron from the nucleus, emitted when a neutron in the nucleus changes to a proton and an electron. Its relative mass is 0 and its relative charge is −1. We represent it as $^{\,0}_{-1}\beta$.

The proton stays in the nucleus so the atomic number goes up by one and the mass number is unchanged. The electron is instantly emitted.

For example, carbon-14 emits a beta particle when it becomes nitrogen.

▶ **2** *What is the relative charge of a beta particle?*

- When a nucleus emits gamma radiation there is no change in the atomic number or the mass number. A gamma ray is an electromagnetic wave released from the nucleus. It has no charge and no mass.

Key words: ion, isotope, atomic number, mass number

Student Book
pages 242–243

P2

6.4 More about alpha, beta and gamma radiation

- When nuclear radiation travels through a material it will collide with the atoms of the material.
- This knocks electrons off them, creating ions. This is called **ionisation**.
- Ionisation in a living cell can damage or kill the cell.
- **Alpha particles** are relatively large, so they have lots of collisions with atoms – they are strongly ionising.
- Because of these collisions, the alpha particles do not penetrate far into a material.
- They can be stopped by a thin sheet of paper, human skin or a few centimetres of air.
- Alpha particles have a positive charge and are deflected by **electric and magnetic fields**.
- **Beta particles** are much smaller and faster than alpha particles so they are less ionising and penetrate further.
- They are blocked by a few metres of air or a thin sheet of aluminium.
- Beta particles have a negative charge and are deflected by electric and magnetic fields in the opposite direction to alpha particles.
- **Gamma rays** are electromagnetic waves so they will travel a long way through a material before colliding with an atom.
- They are weakly ionising and very penetrating.
- Several centimetres of lead or several metres of concrete are needed to absorb most of the radiation.
- Gamma rays are not deflected by electric and magnetic fields.

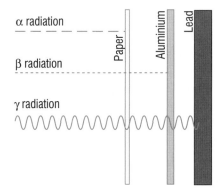

The penetrating powers of α, β and γ radiation

1 *Which type of nuclear radiation is the least penetrating?*
2 *Which type of nuclear radiation is the least ionising?*

Key word: ionisation

6.5 Half-life

Key points

- The half-life of a radioactive isotope is the average time it takes for the number of nuclei of the isotope in a sample to halve.
- The activity of a radioactive source is the number of nuclei that decay per second.
- The number of atoms of a radioactive isotope and the activity both decrease by half every half-life.

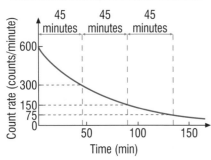

Radioactive decay: a graph of count rate against time

- We can measure the radioactivity of a sample of a radioactive material by measuring the **count rate** from it.
- The radioactivity of a sample decreases over time. How quickly the count rate falls to nearly zero depends on the isotope. Some take a few minutes, others take millions of years.

▐▐▶ **1** *What happens to the count rate of a radioactive sample over time?*

- We use the idea of **half-life** to measure how quickly the radioactivity decreases. It is the time taken for the count rate from the original isotope to fall to half its initial value.
- Or we can define it as the time it takes for the number of unstable nuclei in a sample to halve.
- The half-life is the same for any sample of a particular isotope.

▐▐▶ **2** *What has happened to the original count rate of a radioactive sample after two half-lives have passed?*

Key word: half-life

6.6 Radioactivity at work

Key points

- The use we can make of a radioactive isotope depends on its half-life, and the type of radiation it gives out.
- For radioactive dating of a sample, we need a radioactive isotope that is present in the sample which has a half-life about the same as the age of the sample.

Bump up your grade

For each type of radiation you should know an application, why a particular source is used and the approximate half-life.

- **Alpha sources** are used in smoke alarms. The alpha particles are not dangerous because they are very poorly penetrating. The source needs a half-life of several years.
- **Beta sources** are used for **thickness monitoring** in the manufacture of things like paper or metal foil. Alpha particles would be stopped by a thin sheet of paper and all gamma rays would pass through it. The source needs a half-life of many years, so that decreases in count rate are due to changes in the thickness of the paper.
- **Gamma and beta sources** are used as **tracers** in medicine. The source is injected or swallowed by the patient. Its progress around the body is monitored by a detector outside the patient. The source needs a half-life of a few hours so that the patient is not exposed to unnecessary radioactivity.

▐▐▶ **1** *Why isn't an alpha source used as a tracer in medicine?*

- **Radioactive dating** is used to find the age of ancient material. Carbon dating is used to find the age of wood and other organic material. Uranium dating is used to find the age of igneous rocks.

▐▐▶ **2** *Why do medical tracers have half-lives of just a few hours?*

Key words: tracer, radioactive dating

1 What is the effect of pressure on the rate of radioactive decay?

2 What is background radiation?

3 What was Rutherford's alpha particle scattering experiment?

4 What happens to the mass number of a nucleus when it emits a beta particle?

5 What happens to the atomic number of a nucleus when it emits a beta particle?

6 What happens to the mass number of a nucleus when it emits an alpha particle?

7 What happens to the atomic number of a nucleus when it emits an alpha particle?

8 Why is gamma radiation **not** deflected by electric and magnetic fields?

9 What has happened to the number of atoms undergoing nuclear decay in a sample after three half-lives have passed?

10 Why is alpha radiation unsuitable for monitoring the thickness of metal foil?

11 A radioactive isotope has a half-life of seven hours. A sample of the isotope has a mass of 4 milligrams. What mass of the isotope has decayed after 14 hours?

12 A sample of a radioactive isotope contains 100 000 atoms of the isotope. How many atoms of the isotope will remain after three half-lives?

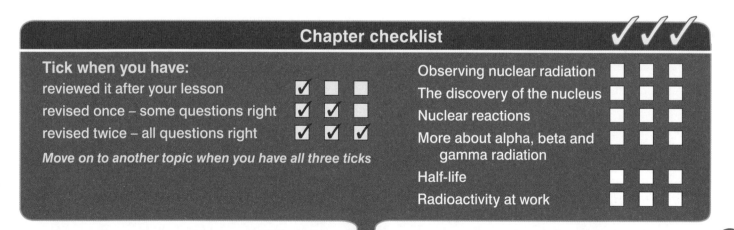

Chapter checklist						
Tick when you have:				Observing nuclear radiation	☐ ☐ ☐	
reviewed it after your lesson	☑ ☐ ☐			The discovery of the nucleus	☐ ☐ ☐	
revised once – some questions right	☑ ☑ ☐			Nuclear reactions	☐ ☐ ☐	
revised twice – all questions right	☑ ☑ ☑			More about alpha, beta and gamma radiation	☐ ☐ ☐	
Move on to another topic when you have all three ticks				Half-life	☐ ☐ ☐	
				Radioactivity at work	☐ ☐ ☐	

7.1 Nuclear fission

- **Nuclear fission** is the splitting of an atomic nucleus.
- There are two fissionable isotopes in common use in nuclear reactors, uranium-235 and plutonium-239. The majority of nuclear reactors use uranium-235.
- Naturally occurring uranium is mostly uranium-238, which is non-fissionable. Most nuclear reactors use 'enriched' uranium that contains 2–3% uranium-235.
- For fission to occur, the uranium-235 or plutonium-239 nucleus must absorb a neutron. The nucleus then splits into two smaller nuclei. In this process two or three neutrons are emitted and energy is released. The energy released in such a nuclear process is much greater than the energy released in a chemical process such as burning.
- A **chain reaction** occurs when each fission event causes further fission events. In a nuclear reactor the process is controlled, so one fission neutron per fission on average goes on to produce further fission.

> 1   *What is enriched uranium?*
> 2   *What happens for fission to occur?*

AQA   *Examiner's tip*

Make sure that you can draw a simple diagram to show a chain reaction.

Key points

- Nuclear fission is the splitting of a nucleus into two approximately equal fragments and the release of two or three neutrons.

- Nuclear fission occurs when a neutron hits a uranium-235 nucleus or a plutonium-239 nucleus and the nucleus splits.

- A chain reaction occurs when neutrons from the fission go on to cause other fission events.

- In a nuclear reactor control rods absorb fission neutrons to ensure that, on average, only one neutron per fission goes on to produce further fission.

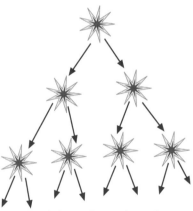

In a chain reaction, each reaction causes more reactions which cause more reactions, etc. etc.

A chain reaction

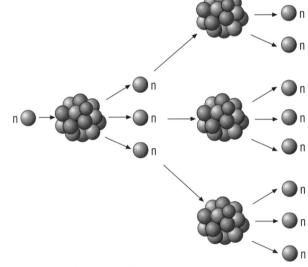

A chain reaction in a nuclear reactor

Key words: nuclear fission, chain reaction

Student Book
pages 252–253 **P2**

7.2 Nuclear fusion

Key points

- Nuclear fusion is the process of forcing two nuclei close enough together so they form a single larger nucleus.

- Energy is released when two light nuclei are fused together.

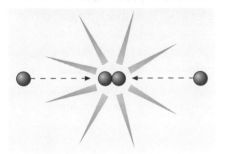

A nuclear fusion reaction

- **Nuclear fusion** is the process of forcing two nuclei close enough together so they form a single larger nucleus.

- Nuclear fusion can be brought about by making two light nuclei collide at very high speed. Fusion is the process by which energy is released in stars.

- There are enormous problems with producing energy from nuclear fusion in reactors. Nuclei approaching each other will repel one another due to their positive charge. To overcome this, the nuclei must be heated to very high temperatures to give them enough energy to overcome the repulsion and fuse. Because of the enormously high temperatures involved, the reaction cannot take place in a normal 'container', but has to be contained by a magnetic field.

>> **1** *By what process is energy released in stars?*
>> **2** *How are nuclei contained in a fusion reactor?*

AQA Examiner's tip

In an examination, students often confuse fission and fusion. Make sure that you can explain the difference between them.

Key word: nuclear fusion

Student Book
pages 254–255 **P2**

7.3 Nuclear issues

Key points

- Radon gas is an α-emitting isotope that seeps into houses in certain areas through the ground.

- There are thousands of fission reactors safely in use throughout the world. None of them are of the same type as the Chernobyl reactors that exploded.

- Nuclear waste is stored in safe and secure conditions for many years after unused uranium and plutonium (to be used in the future) is removed from it.

- The major source of background **radiation** is radon gas which seeps through the ground from radioactive substances in rocks deep underground. Radon gas emits alpha particles, so is a health hazard if breathed in.

- Other sources of background radiation include cosmic rays from outer space, food and drink, air travel, and nuclear weapons testing.

- Medical sources of background radiation include X-rays, as these have an ionising effect, as well as radioactive substances.

>> **1** *What is the major source of background radiation?*

- Uranium and plutonium are chemically removed from used fuel rods from nuclear reactors, as these substances can be used again. The remaining radioactive waste must be stored in secure conditions for many years.

- To reduce exposure to nuclear radiations, workers should:
  - keep as far as possible from sources of radiation–
  - spend as little time exposed as possible
  - shield themselves with materials such as concrete and lead.

>> **2** *Why must radioactive waste be stored securely?*

7.4 The early universe

Key points

- A galaxy is a collection of billions of stars held together by their own gravity.

- Before galaxies and stars formed, the universe was formed of hydrogen and helium.

- The force of gravity pulled matter into galaxies and stars.

- Most scientists believe that the universe was created by the Big Bang about 13 thousand million (13 billion) years ago. At first the universe was a hot glowing ball of radiation. In the first few minutes the nuclei of the lightest elements formed. As the universe expanded, over millions of years, its temperature fell. Uncharged atoms were formed.

▶ **1** *What happened to the temperature of the universe as it expanded?*

- Before galaxies and stars formed, the universe was a dark patchy cloud of hydrogen and helium. Eventually dust and gas were pulled together by **gravitational attraction** to form **stars**. The resulting intense heat started off nuclear fusion reactions in the stars, so they began to emit visible light and other radiation.

- Very large groups of stars are called galaxies. Our Sun is one of the many billions of stars in the Milky Way galaxy. The universe contains billions of galaxies.

- A galaxy is a collection of billions of stars held together by their own gravity. There are billions of galaxies in the universe, with vast empty space between them.

▶ **2** *What is a galaxy?*

Bump up your grade

You should understand that the distance between neighbouring stars is usually millions of times greater than the distance between planets in our Solar System. The distance between neighbouring galaxies is usually millions of times greater than the distance between stars within a galaxy. So the universe is mostly empty space.

Andromeda – the nearest big galaxy to the Milky Way

Key words: gravitational attraction, star

7.5 The life history of a star

- Gravitational forces pull clouds of dust and gas together to form a **protostar**.
- The protostar becomes denser and the nuclei of hydrogen atoms and other light elements start to **fuse** together. Energy is released in the process so the core gets hotter and brighter.
- Stars radiate energy because of hydrogen fusion in the core. This stage can continue for billions of years until the star runs out of hydrogen nuclei. The star is stable because the inward force of gravity is balanced by the outward force of radiation from the core and is called a **main sequence star**.
- Eventually a star runs out of hydrogen nuclei, swells, cools down and turns red.

1   Why are stars in the main sequence stable?

- What happens next in the life cycle of the star depends on its size.
- A star similar in size to our Sun (low mass) is now a **red giant**.
- Helium and other light elements fuse to form heavier elements.
- Fusion stops and the star will contract to form a **white dwarf**.
- Eventually no more light is emitted and the star becomes a **black dwarf**.
- A star much larger than the Sun will swell to become a red **supergiant** which continues to collapse.
- Eventually the star explodes in a **supernova**. The outer layers are thrown out into space. The core is left as a **neutron star**.
- If this is massive enough it becomes a **black hole**. The gravitational field of a black hole is so strong not even light can escape from it.

2   What is a neutron star?

Key points

- A protostar is a gas and dust cloud in space that can go on to form a star.
- Low mass star: protostar → main sequence star → red giant → white dwarf → black dwarf
- High mass star: protostar → main sequence star → red supergiant → supernova → black hole if sufficient mass.
- The Sun will eventually become a black dwarf.
- A supernova is the explosion of a supergiant after it collapses.

AQA *Examiner's tip*

Exam questions may ask you to put the stages of the life cycle of a star in the correct order, so make sure you learn them thoroughly.

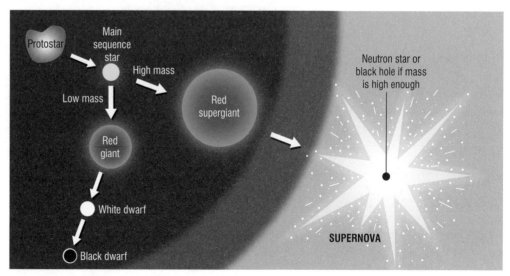

The life cycle of a star

Key words: protostar, main sequence star, red giant, white dwarf, black dwarf, supergiant, supernova, neutron star, black hole

7.6 How the chemical elements formed

● Chemical elements are formed by fusion processes in stars. The nuclei of lighter elements fuse to form the nuclei of heavier elements. The process releases large amounts of energy.

● Elements heavier than iron are only formed in the final stages of the life of a big star. This is because the process requires the input of energy. All the elements get distributed through space by the supernova explosion.

● The presence of the heavier elements in the Sun and inner planets is evidence that they were formed from debris scattered by a supernova.

1 *What is the heaviest element formed by fusion in a main sequence star?*

2 *How are the chemical elements distributed through space?*

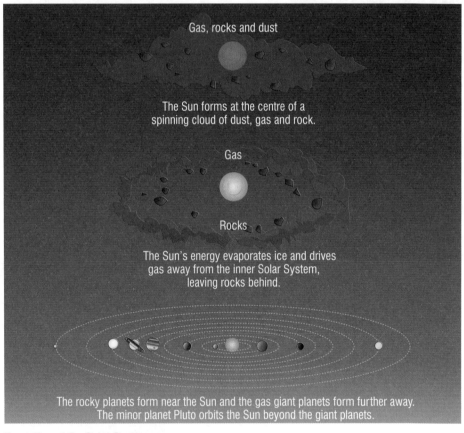

Gas, rocks and dust

The Sun forms at the centre of a spinning cloud of dust, gas and rock.

Gas

Rocks

The Sun's energy evaporates ice and drives gas away from the inner Solar System, leaving rocks behind.

The rocky planets form near the Sun and the gas giant planets form further away. The minor planet Pluto orbits the Sun beyond the giant planets.

Formation of the Solar System

1 What is a fissionable isotope?

2 Which two fissionable isotopes are used in nuclear reactors?

3 When does a chain reaction occur?

4 What is nuclear fusion?

5 How can nuclei be made to come close enough to fuse?

6 How long did it take for the temperature of the universe to fall enough so that uncharged atoms were formed?

7 Why is a black hole black?

8 When is a black hole formed?

9 What will the final stage in the life cycle of the Sun be?

10 What evidence is there that the Sun and inner planets formed from the remnants of a supernova?

11 What is the name of the process that produces the chemical elements?

12 When are elements heavier than iron formed?

Chapter checklist ✓ ✓ ✓

Tick when you have:

	✓	✓	✓
reviewed it after your lesson	✓	☐	☐
revised once – some questions right	✓	✓	☐
revised twice – all questions right	✓	✓	✓

Move on to another topic when you have all three ticks

	✓	✓	✓
Nuclear fission	☐	☐	☐
Nuclear fusion	☐	☐	☐
Nuclear issues	☐	☐	☐
The early universe	☐	☐	☐
The life history of a star	☐	☐	☐
How the chemical elements formed	☐	☐	☐

1 A student sets up the series circuit shown in the diagram.

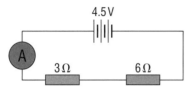

a What is the reading on the ammeter in amperes? Write down the equation you use. Show clearly how you work out your answer and give the unit. (*4 marks*)

b What is the current through
   i   the 3 Ω resistor (*1 mark*)
   ii   the 6 Ω resistor? (*1 mark*)

c What is the potential difference across
   i   the 3 Ω resistor (*1 mark*)
   ii   the 6 Ω resistor? (*1 mark*)

d The student wants to connect a voltmeter to the circuit to measure the potential difference across the 6 Ω resistor. Add the correct symbol to the diagram to show how the student should connect the voltmeter. (*2 marks*)

AQA **Examiner's tip**

Remember that voltmeters are always connected in parallel.

2 *In this question you will be assessed on using good English, organising information clearly and using specialist terms where appropriate.*

Stars form from clouds of dust and gas. Gravitational forces make the clouds become increasingly dense, forming a protostar.

Describe the life cycle of a star, the size of our Sun, from its beginning as a protostar to its final stage as a black dwarf. Include in your explanation how the star produces energy. (*6 marks*)

AQA **Examiner's tip**

All stars produce energy by the process of fusion.

3 A food processor is connected to the 230 V mains supply.
   a The power of the food processor is 950 W.
      What is the current through the food processor? Write down the equation you use. Show clearly how you work out your answer and give the unit. (*3 marks*)

   b 3 A, 10 A and 13 A fuses are available.
      State and explain what size fuse should be used in the plug for the food processor. (*2 marks*)

AQA **Examiner's tip**

The fuse needs to be big enough to allow the normal working current to flow, so calculate the current and choose the fuse with the next largest value.

   c When the food processor is used to make a cake mixture, 738 C of charge flows through the food processor. How long, in minutes, does it take to make the cake mixture? Write down the equation you use. Show clearly how you work out your answer and give the unit. (*4 marks*)

4 A car starts from rest and is driven along a straight, level road. The graph shows how the velocity of the car changes with time for the first 20 s of its journey.

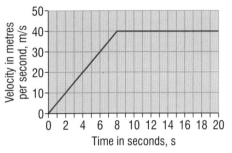

a Use the graph to calculate the acceleration of the car during the first 8 s. Show clearly how you work out your answer and give the unit. *(3 marks)*

b Use the graph to calculate how far the car travels during the first 20 s of its journey. Show clearly how you work out your answer and give the unit. *(3 marks)*

c The car has a mass of 1100 kg.

Calculate the kinetic energy of the car 20 s after it starts its journey. Write down the equation you use. Show clearly how you work out your answer and give the unit. *(3 marks)*

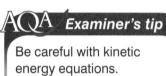
Examiner's tip

Be careful with kinetic energy equations. Remember to square *V*.

5 A skydiver jumps from a plane. The skydiver is shown in the diagram.

a Arrows X and Y represent two forces acting on the skydiver as she falls through the air. Force Y is the weight of the skydiver.

    i The mass of the skydiver is 70 kg. Calculate the weight of the skydiver. Write down the equation you use. Show clearly how you work out your answer and give the unit. *(3 marks)*

    ii What causes force X? *(1 mark)*

b The graph shows how the velocity of the skydiver varies with time as the skydiver falls.

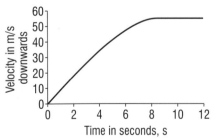

Explain, with reference to the sizes of the forces X and Y, how the velocity of the skydiver varies with time between

    i 0 and 8 seconds *(3 marks)*

    ii 8 and 12 seconds. *(3 marks)*

Answers

B2 Answers

1 Cells, tissues and organs

1.1
1 Mitochondrion (ia)

1.2
1 One bacterium is very tiny. Many bacteria massed together in a colony can be seen.

1.3
1 Mitochondria release energy which muscles need for movement.

1.4
1 The concentration on either side of the membrane.

1.5
1 Enzymes or hormones

1.6
1 In the small intestine

Answers to end of chapter questions

1 Cell membrane, cytoplasm, nucleus, mitochondria, ribosomes
2 Cell wall, chloroplasts, permanent vacuole filled with sap
3 In the cytoplasm
4 Three of: salivary gland, pancreas, stomach, liver, small intestine, large intestine
5 Bile
6 Leaf cells have chloroplasts and a cellulose cell wall. Yeast does not have chloroplasts and no cellulose in its wall.
7 If two solutions are separated by a cell membrane, particles will move from a region of high concentration to a region of low concentration. Gases will also diffuse through the air from a region of high concentration to a region of low concentration.
8 When cells start to divide they are very similar. As the tissues develop the cells change to form particular cells with particular functions.
9 The leaf has mesophyll tissue. The mesophyll cells contain chloroplasts which can photosynthesise.
10 The insoluble food is mixed with digestive juices produced by glands. It is digested in the stomach and small intestine. Bile produced by the liver is added to the food to help digestion. Absorption of the soluble food takes place in the small intestine. Water is absorbed by the large intestine.

2 Organisms in the environment

2.1
1 Sunlight, although artificial light can also be used in experiments

2.2
1 When the temperature falls the enzymes work slower.
2 The variable that is being measured – the measurement depends on what is done with the independent variable.

2.3
1 Starch, fats and oils

2.4
1 Light, temperature and carbon dioxide

2.5
1 Very few plants grow there – those that do are very small, so there is little food for animals.

2.6
1 A square frame which may be divided into a grid

2.7
1 Only the independent variable should affect the results, all other variables must be controlled.

Answers to end of chapter questions

1 Iodine solution
2 The regions containing starch will turn blue-black. Regions without starch will look yellowy-brown.
3 carbon dioxide + water $\xrightarrow{\text{light energy}}$ glucose + oxygen
4 Three of: temperature, availability of nutrients, water, oxygen, carbon dioxide, amount of water
5 It will be hot enough anyway, so it would be a waste of energy. The rate of photosynthesis may stop if the temperature becomes too high.
6 Factors, such as light, temperature and carbon dioxide, which might prevent the rate of photosynthesis increasing above a certain point
7 A line is marked between two points and then the quadrat is placed at regular intervals along the line. The organisms in the quadrat are counted.
8 The mean (average) is the total of all the readings divided by the number of readings. The median is the middle value of the range.
9 There are so many variables which are difficult to control.
10 A measurement is reproducible if the investigation is repeated by another person, or by using different equipment or techniques, and the same results are obtained.

3 Enzymes

3.1
1 Long chains of amino acids

3.2
1 The protein/enzyme changes shape and will stop working.

3.3
1 Amylase

3.4
1 In the liver

3.5
1 Isomerase

3.6
1 Water from dishwashers and washing machines passes into the sewage system and may eventually reach the rivers.

Answers to end of chapter questions

1 Temperature and pH
2 Salivary glands, pancreas and the small intestine
3 Fatty acids and glycerol
4 Hydrochloric acid
5 Bile neutralises acid from the stomach when food passes into the small intestine.
6 The protease pre-digests protein so the baby can absorb it more easily.
7 **Two of**: builds large molecules from small molecules, changes one molecule into another, breaks down large molecules into small molecules.
8 The molecules have more energy so they move around faster and collide more often and more vigorously so there are more frequent collisions in a given time.
9 Advantage: Less energy or expensive equipment is needed because the reactions can take place at normal temperature and pressure. Disadvantage: Costly to produce, denatured at high temperatures.
10 The enzymes speed up the digestion of stains from food, blood and grass, plus lower temperatures can be used in washing machines.

4 Energy from respiration

4.1
1 In the mitochondria

4.2
1 Glucose

Answers to end of chapter questions

1 Using oxygen
2 Respiration without using oxygen
3 Energy
4 Carbon dioxide and water
5 Glycogen
6 glucose + oxygen → carbon dioxide + water (+energy)
7 Lactic acid builds up in the muscles.
8 The breathing rate and heart rate increase.
9 This allows an increased blood supply to the muscle cells to provide oxygen and glucose more quickly and to remove carbon dioxide faster.
10 The amount of oxygen needed to breakdown the lactic acid produced in anaerobic respiration [H]

5 Simple inheritance in animals and plants

5.1
1 Mitosis

5.2
1 Sex cells or gametes, eggs and sperm
2 There are two sets of cell division. A body cell divides into two and each divides again. [H]

5.3
1 Bone marrow

5.4
1 Mendel
2 The order of amino acids in a protein [H]

5.5
1 X and Y
2 This is a description of the physical characteristics. [H]

5.6
1 Polydactyly
2 50%, as one parent (cc) has to pass on the allele, the other parent (Cc) has a 50% risk of passing it on; the child is either Cc or cc. [H]

5.7
1 Tests are carried out on the embryo to diagnose possible disorders.

Answers to end of chapter questions

1 To produce identical cells for growth and to replace cells
2 23 pairs (or 46)
3 Meiosis
4 DNA
5 Different forms of a gene
6 The genetic material from two parents is brought together when the sperm and egg nuclei fuse.
7 They are produced by mitosis. Cells from one parent divide to produce identical cells.
8 The types of genes present in the cells. [H]
9 The individual has one dominant and one recessive allele for a condition. [H]
10 50%, as the dominant gene controls the condition; a child has a 50:50 chance of inheriting the allele from the heterozygous parent. [H]

6 Old and new species

6.1
1 **One of**: bones, teeth, shells, claws
2 Due to geological activity which breaks them up or wears them away.

6.2
1 It eats all the animals.

6.3
1 A new disease being introduced into the population. It is unlikely to be a new predator because dinosaurs were at the top of the food chain.

6.4
1 Islands break away from the mainland, new rivers form, mountain ranges or craters separate them.
2 The wide range of alleles that control the characteristics in a population

Answers to end of chapter questions

1 About 4.5 billion years
2 About 3.5 billion years ago
3 It is possible to date the rocks so the fossils are the same age as the rocks they are preserved in.
4 Early life forms were soft-bodied and did not form fossils.
5 3×10^9
6 The original species may be left with too little to eat.
7 **Two of**: by hunting them for food, by removing the habitat of the species, through polluting the environment, by introducing new competitors to the species, by accidently introducing a new disease
8 A giant asteroid colliding with Earth; Due to sea ice melting and cooling the sea temperature by about 9 °C
9 Two populations of an organism become separated and live in two different regions, e.g. two sides of a new river, either side of a mountain range.
10 reference to isolation of two groups; there is genetic variation in the two populations; alleles are selected which give an advantage; interbreeding no longer possible (as populations diverge/become different); therefore new species are formed (speciation) [H]

Answers to examination-style questions

1 **a** They are produced in cells
to speed up reactions (2 marks)
b i Lipase digests fat/oil, the products are fatty acids and glycerol (3 marks)

ii Protease digests protein
the products are amino acids (2 marks)
c Enzymes denature at higher temperatures and will stop working (2 marks)
2 **a** Stem cells are unspecialised cells which can turn into other cells **or** cells which have not differentiated (2 marks)
b Embryo cells can turn into all types of body cell; bone marrow develops into a limited number of cell types/only blood cells (2 marks)
c By triggering the stem cells to turn into nerve cells (1 mark)
d **One of**: the embryo cannot give permission/embryos are destroyed (1 mark)
3 **a** From fossil evidence (1 mark)
b Lack of light
so plants could not grow
no food for animals/disruption of the base of the food chain (3 marks)
c **Two of**: introduction of a new predator
introduction of a new competitor
a new disease
loss of habitat/food supply
environmental/climate change (2 marks)
d Marks awarded for this answer will be determined by the standard of the scientific response as well as the Quality of Written Communication (QWC).
There is a clear, balanced and detailed explanation of speciation starting with isolation, including a reference to genetic variation and natural selection and ending with speciation, including points from the examples below. The answer shows almost faultless spelling, punctuation and grammar. It is coherent and in an organised, logical sequence. It contains a range of appropriate or relevant specialist terms used accurately. (5–6 marks)
There is some attempt to explain speciation which shows an understanding of isolation and includes a reference to either genetic variation or natural selection with some points from the examples below. There are some errors in spelling, punctuation and grammar. The answer has some structure and organisation. The use of specialist terms has been attempted, but not always accurately. (3–4 marks)
There is some understanding of speciation, with at least one point from the examples below. The spelling, punctuation and grammar are very weak. The answer is poorly organised with almost no specialist terms and/or their use demonstrating a general lack of understanding of their meaning. (1–2 marks)
No relevant content. (0 marks)

Examples of biology points made in the response:
- two populations of a species may become separated/idea of geographical separation
- populations have a wide range of alleles (allow genes)
- this leads to variation (of characteristics) in the population
- some characteristics may be beneficial
- natural selection
- organisms survive to breed
- if the populations stay separate/idea that separation maybe for a long time
- they become too different
- can no longer interbreed/speciation.

4 **a i** 1 (allow 8)
ii 6
iii 8 (allow 7) (3 marks)
b i C
ii A
iii b (3 marks)
c Alleles (1 mark)
d i Asexual reproduction
ii White (2 marks)

C2 Answers

1 Structure and bonding

1.1
1 It is made of non-metals
2 KBr, Na_2O, MgO
3 Lithium atoms lose an electron to form a lithium ion that has a positive charge or Li^+; fluorine atoms gain an electron to form a fluoride ion that has a negative charge or F^-.

1.2
1 Sodium ions have a single positive charge –they are Na^+, and magnesium ions have a double positive charge: they are Mg^{2+} (chloride ions have a single negative charge and are Cl^-)
2 Diagram of sodium atom showing one electron, chlorine atom with seven electrons, sodium ion with no electrons and positive charge, chloride ion with eight electrons and a negative charge.

1.3
1 CaF_2, Na_2SO_4, $Mg(NO_3)_2$, $CuCl_2$, $Fe(OH)_3$

1.4
1 Cl–Cl, H–Cl, H–S–H, O=O, O=C=O

1.5
1 In a giant structure, closely packed together in layers with a regular pattern.
2 Electrostatic forces between positive (metal) ions and delocalised electrons.

Answers to end of chapter questions

1 A substance made of two or more elements that have reacted together or that are chemically bonded together.
2 **a** Outer electrons (electrons in the highest occupied energy level or outer shell).
b They are transferred or metal atoms lose electrons and non-metal atoms gain electrons.
c They are shared. For for each covalent bond one pair of electrons is shared.
3 **a** They lose their one outer electron (one electron in the highest occupied energy level or outer shell).
b They gain one electron so their outer shell has eight electrons or so they have the structure of a noble gas.
4 H_2O, C_2H_6, CO_2,
5 The atoms in copper are all the same size, they are spherical, they are closely packed together (in a giant structure).
6 LiCl, Na_2O, CaF_2, $Mg(OH)_2$, Na_2SO_4, $Ca(NO_3)_2$
7 The attractive forces between oppositely charged ions act in all directions, so the ions pack closely together in a regular arrangement (lattice), ions are very small so a crystal contains many ions.
8 Central C with four shared pairs of electrons (o x) around it and an H outside each of the pairs of electrons.
9 F–F, O=O, H–Br, H–O–H, N with three lines each to an H
10 Diagram of a potassium atom showing one electron, fluorine atom with seven electrons, potassium ion with no electrons and positive charge, fluoride ion with eight electrons and a negative charge
11 Silicon atoms form four covalent bonds, each silicon atom can join to four others, the bonds are strong; this continues so that a giant structure is formed.
12 The outer electrons delocalise, leaving a lattice of positive ions; the delocalised electrons attract the positive ions; the electrostatic forces are strong, and these hold the ions in position. [H]

2 Structure and properties

⫸ 2.1

1 They have giant structures with strong electrostatic forces that hold the ions together and a lot of energy is needed to overcome the forces.
2 The ions can move freely and carry the charge.

⫸ 2.2

1 The molecules in petrol have no overall charge.
2 The intermolecular forces are greater for larger molecules. [H]

⫸ 2.3

1 Every atom is joined to several other atoms, many strong covalent bonds have to be broken and so it takes a large amount of energy to melt the giant structure.
2 Similarities: forms of carbon; giant covalent structures or covalent bonding. Differences: carbon atoms in diamond are bonded to four other carbon atoms, only to three other atoms in graphite; diamond is three-dimensional, graphite two-dimensional; diamond is hard, graphite is slippery/soft; diamond is transparent, graphite is grey/opaque; graphite is a good conductor of heat/electricity, diamond is a poor conductor; graphite has delocalised electrons, diamond does not; graphite has intermolecular forces, diamond does not.
3 Similarities: forms of carbon, hexagonal rings of atoms. Differences: graphite is a giant structure, fullerenes are molecules; graphite is two-dimensional, fullerenes are three-dimensional/cage-like; graphite forms large particles, many fullerenes are nano-sized.

⫸ 2.4

1 When stretched, the atoms slide into new positions without breaking apart.
2 They are harder than pure metals; they can be made/designed to have specific properties or special properties such as shape memory alloys.
3 Delocalised electrons move rapidly through the metal structure.

⫸ 2.5

1 They are made using different reaction conditions; they have different structures or differently shaped molecules.
2 Thermosoftening polymers have no cross-links or no covalent bonds between the polymer chains, thermosetting polymers have cross-links.
3 The weak intermolecular forces between the chains (are overcome by heating). [H]

⫸ 2.6

1 A very small particle that is a few nanometres in size, or made of a few hundreds of atoms
2 Its effects on people and the environment should be researched/tested (to ensure it is safe to use).

Answers to end of chapter questions

1 It has a giant ionic structure with strong electrostatic forces/bonds that hold the ions firmly in position and that need a lot of energy to overcome/break them.
2 They are made of small molecules or covalent bonds act only between the atoms within a molecule.
3 Different monomers change the structure of the polymer chains or the polymer chains have different shapes/structures.
4 An alloy (mixture of metals) that can be bent/deformed and changes back to its original shape when heated.
5 Every carbon atom is covalently/strongly bonded to four other carbon atoms in a giant (3-D) covalent structure.

6 The ions cannot move in the solid, but become free to move in the molten liquid or in solution.
7 The atoms are in layers. The layers slide over each other, into the new shape, without breaking apart.
8 a They are very much smaller, have a much greater surface area.
   b They are more effective (because of their greater surface area), needs to use much less silver (so it is cheaper), easier to attach to sock fibres.
9 They do not soften/melt when they get hot, they are good insulators (of heat), they can be moulded into shape but then are rigid/hard.
10 The outer electrons delocalise, leaving a lattice of positive ions; the delocalised electrons strongly attract the positive ions and hold them in position. [H]
11 There are delocalised electrons in graphite or one electron from each carbon atom is delocalised; the delocalised electrons carry the electrical charge. [H]
12 Forces between molecules (that are much weaker than covalent bonds within the molecules) [H]
13 Forms of carbon, with large molecules, based on hexagonal rings of carbon atoms, often cage-like structures, can be nano-sized, have many useful applications [H]

3 How much?

⫸ 3.1

1 The mass of an electron is very small compared to that of a proton or neutron.
2 9 protons, 9 electrons, 10 neutrons
3 Atoms of the same element or atoms with the same atomic/proton number that have different numbers of neutrons

⫸ 3.2

1 23 g
2 It has (two main) isotopes and the relative atomic mass is an average value.
3 $(23 \times 2) + 32 + (16 \times 4) = 142$
4 $24 + 12 + (16 \times 3) = 84g$ (must have g)

⫸ 3.3

1 $(12/16) \times 100 = 75\%$
2 $70/56 = 1.25 : 30/16 = 1.875$, 1:1.5, 2:3, empirical formula Fe_2O_3

⫸ 3.4

1 $CaCO_3 = 100$, $CaO = 56$, one mole $CaCO_3$ gives one mole of CaO or 100g $CaCO_3$ gives 56g CaO, 10g $CaCO_3$ gives $(10/100) \times 56 = 5.6g$

⫸ 3.5

1 $2Ca + O_2 \rightarrow 2CaO$, 80g $Ca \rightarrow 112g$ CaO, 4g $Ca \rightarrow 5.6g$ CaO, $(4.4/5.6) \times 100 = 78.6\%$
2 Reactions may not go to completion, other reactions may happen, some product may be lost when separated or collected.
3 To help conserve resources, reduce waste and/or pollution.

⫸ 3.6

1 A reaction that can go both forwards and backwards, or both ways or in both directions.

⫸ 3.7

1 Paper chromatography

⫸ 3.8

1 To separate the compounds (in the mixture)
2 From the molecular ion peak or the peak with the largest mass (furthest to the right in the spectrum)

Answers to end of chapter questions

1 a Isotopes
   b 35/17 Cl has two fewer neutrons than 37/17 Cl (18 neutrons compared with 20 neutrons).
2 Reversible

3 (Artificial) colours
4 62
5 102g
6 51.4% (51%)
7 **Two from:** magnesium oxide was lost or not collected, the magnesium did not all react, magnesium reacted with other substances in air.
8 V_2O_5 [H]
9 13.6g [H]
10 75% [H]
11 Relative molecular mass (of the compound) [H]

4 Rates and energy

⫸ 4.1

1 Amount (of reactant or product) and time
2 The gradient of the line at a given time gives the rate at that time.

⫸ 4.2

1 Activation energy
2 Increasing: temperature, concentration of solutions, pressure of gases, surface area of solids; using a catalyst
3 Powders have greater surface area than large lumps of solid, and this increases the chance of collisions.

⫸ 4.3

1 It increases the frequency of collisions and the energy of the particles.

⫸ 4.4

1 It increases the frequency of collisions.
2 The frequency of collisions increases because there are more molecules in the same volume.

⫸ 4.5

1 They remain at the end of a reaction or they are not used up in the reaction.
2 Catalysts often work with only one type of reaction.

⫸ 4.6

1 They reduce the energy needed and the time needed, and so reduce costs. They may reduce the amount of fossil fuel used and so conserve resources and reduce pollution.
2 They may be toxic or expensive.
3 Nanoscience and enzymes

⫸ 4.7

1 It transfers energy to the surroundings or heats the surroundings.
2 Either it cools the surroundings or it needs to be heated to keep it going.

⫸ 4.8

1 It is an endothermic reaction.
2 It is an exothermic reaction.

⫸ 4.9

1 One advantage e.g. less waste, less materials/resources used; one disadvantage e.g. has to be heated or needs energy so it can be used again, slower reaction, smaller temperature rise.
2 One advantage e.g. can be used anywhere, can be stored easily (ice needs to be made and/or stored in special equipment); one disadvantage e.g. can only be used once, more waste, possibly more hazardous than ice.

Answers to end of chapter questions

1 Increase concentration of acid, increase temperature, use powdered zinc, use a catalyst
2 From the gradient or slope of the line
3 The minimum energy that particles must have for collisions to produce a reaction
4 Two examples e.g. combustion, oxidation, neutralisation
5 (Thermal decomposition is) an endothermic reaction
6 High temperature, high pressure, catalyst

7 Particles are closer together (more particles in the same volume), so collisions are more frequent (more collisions per second).

8 Particles collide more frequently, and with more energy so more collisions have the activation energy (minimum energy needed for reaction).

5 Salts and electrolysis

▶ 5.1
1 Hydrogen ions, $H^+(aq)$
2 A soluble base or a substance that produces hydroxide ions in solution, $OH^-(aq)$
3 Universal indicator or full-range indicators

▶ 5.2
1 Any metal that is more reactive than hydrogen, but less reactive than calcium, e.g. lead, tin, iron, aluminium, magnesium.
2 To use up all of the acid or to neutralise all of the acid
3 a Magnesium nitrate and hydrogen
  b Copper chloride and water

▶ 5.3
1 Water, H_2O
2 Zinc carbonate would be produced as a precipitate or solid, sodium sulfate would remain in the solution.

▶ 5.4
1 They must be melted or dissolved in water.
2 a Chlorine
  b Zinc

▶ 5.5
1 Reduction or positive sodium ions gain electrons
2 $2Cl^- \rightarrow Cl_2 + 2e^-$ [H]
3 a Oxygen
  b Copper

▶ 5.6
1 To lower the melting temperature
2 Aluminium and carbon dioxide

▶ 5.7
1 The solution contains hydrogen ions which are discharged in preference to sodium ions because sodium is more reactive than hydrogen.
2 Its (three) products have many uses or can be used in many ways.

▶ 5.8
1 To make them look attractive, to protect the metal from corrosion, to reduce the cost (of making the items from pure silver).
2 Pass electricity through a cell with the item of jewellery as the negative electrode, the positive electrode made of silver and containing a solution of a silver salt (e.g. silver nitrate solution) (as the electrolyte).

Answers to end of chapter questions

1 a An alkali
  b Neutralisation
  c There is no visible change and it will show when the pH is 7.
  d nitric acid + sodium hydroxide → sodium nitrate + water
2 Add zinc oxide, a little at a time, to dilute sulfuric acid, until there is an excess, filter off the excess, evaporate some of the water, leave to cool and crystallise.
3 Mix the two solutions, filter the mixture or leave to settle and decant or centrifuge and decant to separate the solid (precipitate). Then wash with distilled water and dry.
4 Less expensive than pure gold, to improve appearance, so they do not corrode (or cause allergic reactions)
5 Hydrogen, chlorine and sodium hydroxide. A use for each, e.g. hydrogen: to make hydrochloric

acid, margarine manufacture, fuel; chlorine: to make bleach, plastics; sodium hydroxide: to make soap, paper, as a cleaning agent (ovens/drains)

6 a It needs: large amounts of electricity, high temperature to melt the aluminium oxide.
  b To lower the melting/operating temperature (of the electrolyte)
7 At the negative electrode: sodium ions gain electrons, are reduced, to sodium atoms/metal. At the positive electrode: chloride ions lose electrons, are oxidised, to chlorine atoms, which form chlorine molecules/gas.
8 At the negative electrode: $2H^+ + 2e^- \rightarrow H_2$
At the positive electrode: $2Cl^- \rightarrow Cl_2 + 2e^-$ [H]

Answers to examination-style questions

1 a Li – metallic, F_2 – covalent, LiF – ionic
  (3 marks)
  b F_2 *(1 mark)*
  c i Li *(1 mark)*
    ii Li *and* LiF *(1 mark)*
  d i

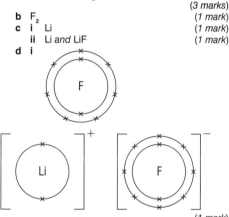

  (1 mark)
    ii Li at centre of one circle with two crosses with brackets and + sign top right outside bracket
    F at centre of two concentric circles with two crosses on inner circle and eight crosses on outer circle enclosed in brackets with – sign top right outside brackets *(4 marks)*
  e i A particle that is a few nm (nanometres) in size or containing a few hundred atoms *(1 mark)*
    ii Much larger surface area, react much faster or more easily, or other different property *(1 mark)*
  f The electrons in the highest energy level (outer shell)
    are delocalised
    and attract or hold the positive metal ions together
    by strong electrostatic forces [H] *(4 marks)*
2 a 136 (no units) *(2 marks)*
    if incorrect: $40 + 1 + 31 + (4 \times 16)$ gains 1 mark
  b 29.4% *(2 marks)*
    allow error carried forward from **a**; if answer incorrect: correct working (40/136) or answer to **a** ×100 gains 1 mark
  c $CaCO_3$ contains more
    Working: either $(40/100) \times 100\% = 40\%$ Ca
    or CO_3 (60) $< HPO_4$ (96) *(2 marks)*
  d Isotopes are atoms of the same element or atoms with the same number of protons with different numbers of neutrons or different mass numbers
    $^{31}_{15}P$ has 16 neutrons, $^{32}_{15}P$ has 17 neutrons *(3 marks)*
  e Mass in 100g = 43.7g P : 56.3g O
    Moles of atoms = 43.7/31 : 56.3/16 (divide by A_r)

Ratio of atoms = 1.41 : 3.52
Divide by 1.41 = 1 : 2.5
Simplest ratio = 2 : 5, so empirical formula is P_2O_5 *(4 marks)*
3 a It is reversible. *(1 mark)*
  b N with 3H at least 90° apart, with xo between each H and N (1) and xx close to N giving a total of 8 electrons around N *(1 mark)*

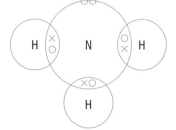

  c It produces $OH^-(aq)$. *(1 mark)*
  d i $H^+(aq) + OH^-(aq) \rightarrow H_2O(l)$ *(1 mark)*
    ii Neutralisation *(1 mark)*
    iii Marks awarded for this answer will be determined by the standard of the scientific response as well as the Quality of Written Communication (QWC).
    There is a clear, logical and detailed scientific description of how to make ammonium nitrate crystals including an appropriate risk assessment. The answer shows almost faultless spelling, punctuation and grammar. It is coherent and in an organised, logical sequence. It contains a range of appropriate and relevant specialist terms used accurately. *(5–6 marks)*
    There is a scientific description of how to make ammonium nitrate crystals and an attempt at risk assessment. There are some errors in spelling, punctuation and grammar. The answer has some structure and organisation. The use of specialist terms has been attempted, but not always accurately. *(3–4 marks)*
    There is a brief description of how to make ammonium nitrate but a risk assessment may be missing. The spelling, punctuation and grammar are very weak. The answer is poorly organised with almost no specialist terms and/or their use demonstrating a general lack of understanding of their meaning. *(1–2 marks)*
    No relevant content. *(0 marks)*

Examples of chemistry points made in the candidate's response:
- Use UI paper or use pH meter/probe to check pH
- Add ammonia solution to dilute nitric acid
- A little at a time
- Stir or swirl the mixture
- Until indicator changes colour or until excess ammonia or ammonia can be smelled
- Remove indicator (boil with charcoal and filter)
- Heat solution to evaporate some water (and excess ammonia)
- Allow solution to cool and crystallise (allow to evaporate slowly)
- Separate crystals from any remaining solution
- Dilute nitric acid is irritant/corrosive – risk to eyes and skin etc
- Ammonia solution is irritant/corrosive – risk to eyes and skin etc.
- Heating/evaporating solution – risk to eyes and skin etc.
- Wear safety goggles, wipe up spillages, avoid contact with skin and clothes, care when heating.

e i Relative formula masses:
$NH_3 = 17$, $NH_4NO_3 = 80$
Number of moles $NH_3 = 1.7/17 = 0.1$
From equation, number of moles of NH_3 = number of moles of NH_4NO_3 or 17 g NH_3 produces 80 g NH_4NO_3
Mass of 0.1 mole $NH_4NO_3 = 80 \times 0.1 =$ 8 g or 1.7 g NH_3 produces 8 g NH_4NO_3
[H] (3 marks)

ii $(5.2/8.0) \times 100$
= 65%   [H] (2 marks)

4 a Exothermic   (1 mark)
b A substance that speeds up a reaction without being used up in the reaction (2 marks)
c Two from: increase the surface area of iron or use smaller particles/nanoparticles of iron, increase the concentration of salt, increase flow of air e.g. shake or blow on the pack (2 marks)

5 a Chlorine   (1 mark)
b Hydrogen   (1 mark)
c Sodium hydroxide   (1 mark)
d Sodium is more reactive than hydrogen so hydrogen ions are discharged in preference to sodium ions.   (2 marks)
e $2Cl^-(aq) \rightarrow Cl_2(g) + 2e^-$
because chloride ions lose electrons or oxidation is loss of electrons.   [H] (2 marks)

P2 Answers

1 Motion

▶ 1.1
1 Metres, m
2 8 m/s

▶ 1.2
1 Velocity is speed in a particular direction.
2 metres per second squared, m/s^2

▶ 1.3
1 Constant velocity, zero acceleration
2 A straight line with a negative gradient

▶ 1.4
1 **a** Increasing velocity
  b Increasing acceleration

Answers to end of chapter questions
1 20 m/s
2 Straight horizontal line
3 Acceleration
4 A deceleration
5 The gradient increases.
6 By changing its direction.
7 4 m/s^2
8 Area between the line and the x-axis
9 10 m/s
10 20 m/s
11 1 m/s^2 [H]
12 50 m   [H]

2 Forces

▶ 2.1
1 Newton, N
2 Downwards (or towards (the centre of) the Earth)

▶ 2.2
1 Newton, N
2 7 N in the same direction as the two forces

▶ 2.3
1 Acceleration decreases
2 2000 N

▶ 2.4
1 Zero
2 Stopping distance = thinking distance + braking distance

▶ 2.5
1 There is a resultant force acting on it.
2 It will reach a terminal velocity because the resultant force becomes zero.

▶ 2.6
1 An inelastic object is one that does **not** regain its original shape when the forces deforming it are removed.
2 9 N
3 The graph of extension against force applied is no longer a straight line.

▶ 2.7
1 Less engine force and less power are needed to maintain a certain speed. Less fuel is needed so fuel costs are reduced.
2 The vehicle is not accelerating, so the resultant force on it is zero. So the engine force and air resistance are balanced.

Answers to end of chapter questions
1 15 N to the left
2 The object continues to move at a steady speed in the same direction.
3 When the force is in the opposite direction to the motion.
4 The acceleration increases.
5 750 N
6 0.4 m/s^2
7 The faster the speed the greater the stopping distance.
8 The final steady speed of an object falling freely through a fluid.
9 700 N
10 One that goes back to its original size and shape when the force applied to it is removed.
11 The extension is directly proportional to the force applied, provided the limit of proportionality is not exceeded.
12 500 N/m

3 Work, energy and momentum

▶ 3.1
1 Joule, J
2 2400 J

▶ 3.2
1 320 J
2 160 W

▶ 3.3
1 500 J
2 Some elastic potential energy is transferred by heating.

▶ 3.4
1 When they are moving
2 30 000 kg m/s

▶ 3.5
1 The total momentum before the explosion
2 It is equal and opposite.

▶ 3.6
1 Time taken for a collision to take place
2 Cars may be hit from either the front or the rear, in either case the crumple zone reduces the forces on the car (or increases the impact time).

▶ 3.7
1 **a** They continue to move forwards when the car stops and will hit the windscreen.
  b The narrow seatbelt would not spread the force across the passenger's body and might cut them.

Answers to end of chapter questions
1 When a force moves through a distance
2 Work done = energy transferred

3 Watt, W
4 54 J
5 The energy stored in an elastic object when it is stretched or squashed
6 540 000 J
7 kg m/s or Ns
8 50 000 kg m/s
9 The thick foam mat increases the impact time compared with the hard floor, reducing the force on the gymnast.
10 2.0 m   [H]
11 1.3 s   [H]
12 0.6 m/s to the right   [H]

4 Current electricity

▶ 4.1
1 It gains electrons.
2 They will repel each other.

▶ 4.2
1
2
(circuit symbol)

▶ 4.3
1 An ammeter
2 Ohm, Ω

▶ 4.4
1 The resistance of the LDR increases.
2 Reversing the pd has no effect on the current–potential difference curve for the filament bulb.

▶ 4.5
1 There is no complete path for the current, so no current flows.
2 Add all the individual resistances.

▶ 4.6
1 Current cannot flow through that component but it can flow in other parts of the circuit.
2 They are equal.

Answers to end of chapter questions
1 Negative
2 It loses electrons.
3 A repulsive force
4

(circuit diagram)

5 60 Ω
6 4.5 V
7 A conductor that obeys Ohm's law – the current is directly proportional to resistance if the temperature is constant.
8 The resistance in one direction is very high, so there is no current. In the opposite direction the resistance is lower so current will flow.
9 The potential difference across it increases.
10 13 Ω
11 The ammeter should be placed in series and the voltmeter in parallel with the resistor.
12 0.75 A

5 Mains electricity

▶ 5.1
1 Current that passes in one direction only
2 0 V

▶ 5.2
1 Brass is a good conductor and does not rust or oxidise.
2 So that the case cannot become live and electrocute you

⫸ 5.3
1 A thin wire that heats up and melts if too much current passes through it
2 Plastic is an insulator so it cannot become live.

⫸ 5.4
1 3 kW
2 2300 W

⫸ 5.5
1 240 C
2 46 000 J   [H]

⫸ 5.6
1 The case of the hairdryer is plastic, so it doesn't need an earth.
2 They transfer a lot of energy by heating, rather than as light.

Answers to end of chapter questions
1 230 V
2 50 Hz
3 +/– 325 V
4 Blue
5 It has green and yellow stripes.
6 Plastic is a good electrical insulator.
7 3 A
8 Coulomb, C
9 An electromagnetic switch that opens and cuts off the supply if the current is bigger than a certain value.
10 30 000 J
11 10 A
12 12 V   [H]

6 Radioactivity

⫸ 6.1
1 The nucleus
2 It stays the same.

⫸ 6.2
1 Most of the atom is empty space.
2 The nucleus is where most of the mass of the atom is concentrated, very small and positively charged.

⫸ 6.3
1 +2
2 –1

⫸ 6.4
1 Alpha
2 Gamma

⫸ 6.5
1 It decreases.
2 It has decreased to one quarter of its original value.

⫸ 6.6
1 Alpha particles are very poorly penetrating, so they would not be detected outside the body/ Alpha is very ionising so would be damaging to the patient.
2 To allow time to complete the procedure but minimise unnecessary exposure of the patient.

Answers to end of chapter questions
1 It has no effect.
2 Radiation that is around us all the time.
3 Firing alpha particles at a thin metal foil
4 It stays the same.
5 It goes up by 1.
6 It goes down by 4.
7 It goes down by 2.
8 Gamma radiation is uncharged.
9 It has decreased to one-eighth of its original value.
10 Alpha radiation would not be able to pass through the foil, irrespective of thickness.

11 3 milligrams
12 12 500

7 Energy from the nucleus

⫸ 7.1
1 Uranium that contains 2–3% uranium-235
2 A nucleus absorbs a neutron.

⫸ 7.2
1 Fusion
2 In a magnetic field

⫸ 7.3
1 Radon gas
2 So that it does not enter the environment because it remains radioactive

⫸ 7.4
1 It decreased.
2 A collection of billions of stars held together by their own gravity

⫸ 7.5
1 The forces acting on them are balanced.
2 The core left after a supernova explodes

⫸ 7.6
1 Iron
2 By a supernova explosion

Answers to end of chapter questions
1 An isotope that can undergo the process of fission
2 Uranium-235 and plutonium-239
3 When each fission event causes further fission events
4 The process of forcing two nuclei close enough together so they form a single larger nucleus.
5 Nuclear fusion can be brought about by making two light nuclei collide at very high speed.
6 Millions of years
7 Not even light can escape from it.
8 After a supernova, if the star has sufficient mass
9 A black dwarf
10 The presence of the heavier elements in the Sun and inner planets
11 Fusion
12 In a supernova

Answers to examination-style questions

1 a $R = 3\,\Omega + 6\,\Omega = 9\,\Omega$

$I = \dfrac{V}{R}$

$I = 4.5\dfrac{V}{9\,\Omega}$

$I = 0.5\,A$ (4 marks)

  b i 0.5 A   (1 mark)

      ii 0.5 A   (1 mark)

  c i 1.5 V   (1 mark)

      ii 3.0 V   (1 mark)

  d Correct symbol shown in parallel across the 6 Ω resistor   (2 marks)

2 Marks awarded for this answer will be determined by the Quality of Written Communication (QWC) as well as the standard of the scientific response.

There is a clear, balanced and detailed description of the life cycle of a star. The answer shows almost faultless spelling, punctuation and grammar. It is coherent and in an organised, logical sequence. It contains a range of appropriate or relevant specialist terms used accurately.   (5–6 marks)
There is a description of the life cycle of a star. There are some errors in spelling, punctuation and grammar. The answer has some structure

and organisation. The use of specialist terms has been attempted, but not always accurately.   (3–4 marks)
There is a brief description of the life cycle of a star, which has little clarity and detail. The spelling, punctuation and grammar are very weak. The answer is poorly organised with almost no specialist terms and/or their use demonstrating a general lack of understanding of their meaning.   (1–2 marks)
No relevant content.   (0 marks)

Examples of physics points made in the response:
• as the protostar becomes denser, it gets hotter
• the nuclei of hydrogen atoms and other light elements start to fuse together releasing energy in the process
• this stage can continue for billions of years, the star is stable and is called a main sequence star
• eventually the star runs out of hydrogen nuclei
• the star swells, cools down and is now a red giant
• helium and other light elements fuse to form heavier elements
• fusion stops and the star will contract to form a white dwarf
• eventually no more light is emitted and the star becomes a black dwarf.

3 a $I = \dfrac{P}{V}$

$I = \dfrac{950\,W}{230\,V}$

$= 4.1\,A$ (3 marks)

  b Should use 10 A.
3 A too low and would blow as soon as processor switched on, 13 A too big to protect the appliance.   (2 marks)

  c $I = \dfrac{Q}{t}$

$t = \dfrac{Q}{I}$

$= \dfrac{738}{4.1}$

$= 180\,s$

$= \dfrac{180}{60} = 3$ minutes   (4 marks)

4 a Acceleration = gradient

$a = \dfrac{40}{8}$

$= 5.0\,m/s^2$ (3 marks)

  b Distance travelled = area under graph
$s = (0.5 \times 8 \times 40) + (12 \times 40) = 160 + 480$
$= 640\,m$ (3 marks)

  c $E_k = \frac{1}{2} \times m \times v^2$
At 20 s, speed = 40 m/s
$E_k = \frac{1}{2} \times 1100\,kg \times (40\,m/s)^2$
$E_k = 880\,000\,J$ (3 marks)

5 a i $W = m \times g$
$W = 70\,kg \times 10\,N/kg$
$W = 700\,N$ (3 marks)

    ii Air resistance   (1 mark)

  b i Initially X is 0 so the only downward force is Y, so the skydiver accelerates downwards.
Gradient = acceleration, so initial gradient is steepest.
As velocity increases X increases, so acceleration decreases so gradient of line becomes less steep up to $t = 8\,s$.   (3 marks)

    ii At 8 seconds X and Y are equal, so the resultant force is 0,
so the acceleration is 0,
skydiver travels at terminal velocity,
so graph is a horizontal straight line.   (3 marks)

Glossary

A

Acceleration Change of velocity per second (in metres per second per second, m/s^2).

Acid A sour substance that can attack metal, clothing or skin. The chemical opposite of an alkali. When dissolved in water, its solution has a pH number less than 7. Acids are proton (H+ ion) donors.

Activation energy The minimum energy needed to start off a reaction.

Active site The site on an enzyme where the reactants bind.

Algal cells The cells of algae, single-celled or simple multicellular organisms, which can photosynthesise but are not plants.

Alkali Its solution has a pH number more than 7.

Allele A version of a particular gene.

Alpha radiation Alpha particles, each composed of two protons and two neutrons, emitted by unstable nuclei.

Alternating current Electric current in a circuit that repeatedly reverses its direction.

Amino acid The building block of protein.

Amylase The enzyme made in the salivary glands and the pancreas that speeds up the breakdown of starch into simple sugars.

Anhydrous Describes a substance that does not contain water.

Aqueous solution The mixture made by adding a soluble substance to water.

Atomic number The number of protons (which equals the number of electrons) in an atom. It is sometimes called the proton number.

Attract To cause to move nearer.

B

Bacterial colony A population of billions of bacteria grown in culture.

Base The oxide, hydroxide or carbonate of a metal that will react with an acid, forming a salt as one of the products. (If a base dissolves in water it is called an alkali). Bases are proton (H+ ion) acceptors.

Beta radiation Beta particles that are high-energy electrons created in and emitted from unstable nuclei.

Bile Yellowy-green liquid made in the liver and stored in the gall bladder. It is released into the small intestine and emulsifies fats.

Biological detergent Washing detergent that contains enzymes.

Biomass Biological material from living or recently living organisms.

Black dwarf A star that has faded out and gone cold.

Black hole An object in space that has so much mass that nothing, not even light, can escape from its gravitational field.

Braking distance The distance travelled by a vehicle during the time its brakes act.

C

Cable Two or three insulated wires surrounded by an outer layer of rubber or flexible plastic.

Carbohydrase Enzyme that speeds up the breakdown of carbohydrates.

Carrier Individual who is heterozygous for a faulty allele that causes a genetic disease in the homozygous form.

Catalyst A substance that speeds up a chemical reaction. At the end of the reaction the catalyst remains chemically unchanged.

Cell membrane The membrane around the contents of a cell that controls what moves in and out of the cell.

Cell wall A rigid structure that surrounds the cells of living organisms apart from animals.

Cellulose A big carbohydrate molecule that makes up plant and algal cell walls.

Chain reaction Reactions in which one reaction causes further reactions, which in turn cause further reactions, etc. A nuclear chain reaction occurs when fission neutrons cause further fission, so more fission neutrons are released. These go on to produce further fission.

Chlorophyll The green pigment contained in the chloroplasts.

Chloroplast The organelle in which photosynthesis takes place.

Chromatography The process whereby small amounts of dissolved substances are separated by running a solvent along a material such as absorbent paper.

Circuit breaker An electromagnetic switch that opens and cuts the current off if too much current passes through it.

Collision theory An explanation of chemical reactions in terms of reacting particles colliding with sufficient energy for a reaction to take place.

Concentration gradient The gradient between an area where a substance is at a high concentration and an area where it is at a low concentration.

Conservation of momentum In a closed system, the total momentum before an event is equal to the total momentum after the event. Momentum is conserved in any collision or explosion provided no external forces act on the objects that collide or explode.

Covalent bonding The attraction between two atoms that share one or more pairs of electrons.

Crumple zone Region of a vehicle designed to crumple in a collision to reduce the force on the occupants.

Cystic fibrosis A genetic disease that affects the lungs, digestive and reproductive systems. It is inherited through a recessive allele.

Cytoplasm The water-based gel in which the organelles of all living cells are suspended.

D

Deceleration Change of velocity per second when an object slows down.

Delocalised electron Bonding electron that is no longer associated with any one particular atom.

Denatured Change the shape of an enzyme so that it can no longer speed up a reaction.

Differentiate Specialise for a particular function.

Diffusion The net movement of particles of a gas or a solute from an area of high concentration to an area of low concentration (along a concentration gradient).

Digestion Breaking down into small molecules by the digestive enzymes.

Digestive juice The mixture of enzymes and other chemicals produced by the digestive system.

Digestive system The organ system running from the mouth to the anus where food is digested.

Diode Electrical device that allows current flow in one direction only.

Direct current Electric current in a circuit that is in one direction only.

Directly proportional A graph will show this if the line of best fit is a straight line through the origin.

DNA fingerprint Pattern produced by analysing the DNA which can be used to identify an individual.

Dominant The characteristic that will show up in the offspring even if only one of the alleles is inherited.

Dot and cross diagram A drawing to show the arrangement of the outer shell electrons only of the atoms or ions in a substance.

Drag force A force opposing the motion of an object due to fluid (e.g. air) flowing past the object as it moves.

E

Elastic A material is elastic if it is able to regain its shape after it has been squashed or stretched.

Elastic potential energy Energy stored in an elastic object when work is done to change its shape.

Electrolyte A liquid, containing free-moving ions, that is broken down by electricity in the process of electrolysis.

Electron A tiny particle with a negative charge. Electrons orbit the nucleus in atoms or ions.

Empirical formula The simplest ratio of elements in a compound.

Endothermic A reaction that *takes in* energy from the surroundings.

Enzyme A protein molecule that acts as biological catalyst.

Epidermal tissue The tissue of the epidermis – the outer layer of an organism.

Epithelial tissue Tissue made up of relatively unspecialised cells that line the tubes and organs of the body.

Exothermic A reaction that *gives out* energy to the surroundings.

Extinction Extinction is the permanent loss of all the members of a species.

F

Fatty acid Building block of lipids.

Filament bulb Electrical device designed to produce light.

Force A force can change the motion of an object (in newtons, N).

Frequency (of an alternating current) The number of complete cycles an alternating current passes through each second. The unit of frequency is the hertz (Hz).

Friction Force opposing the movement of one surface over another.

Fructose syrup A sugar syrup.

Fullerene Form of the element carbon that can form a large cage-like structure, based on hexagonal rings of carbon atoms.

Fuse A fuse contains a thin wire that melts and cuts the current off if too much current passes through it.

G

Gamma radiation Electromagnetic radiation emitted from unstable nuclei in radioactive substances.

Gas chromatography The process of separating the components in a mixture by passing the vapours through a column and detecting them as they leave the column at different times.

Genetic disorder Disease that is inherited.

Genetic material The DNA that carries the instructions for making a new cell or a new individual.

Geographical isolation This is when two populations become physically isolated by a geographical feature.

Giant covalent structure A huge 3-D network of covalently bonded atoms (e.g. the giant lattice of carbon atoms in diamond or graphite).

Giant lattice A huge 3-D network of atoms or ions (e.g. the giant ionic lattice in sodium chloride).

Giant structure See giant lattice.

Glandular tissue The tissue that makes up the glands and secretes chemicals, e.g. enzymes, hormones.

Glucose A simple sugar.

Glycerol Building block of lipids.

Glycogen Carbohydrate store in animals, including the muscles, liver and brain of the human body.

Gradient Change of the quantity plotted on the y-axis divided by the change of the quantity plotted on the x-axis.

Gravitational attraction Force that pulls two masses together.

Gravitational field strength, g The force of gravity on an object of mass 1 kg (in newtons per kilogram, N/kg).

Gravitational potential energy Energy of an object due to its position in a gravitational field. Near the Earth's surface, change of GPE (in joules, J) = weight (in newtons, N) × vertical distance moved (in metres, m).

H

Half-life (of a radioactive isotope) Average time taken for the number of nuclei of the isotope (or mass of the isotope) in a sample to halve.

Hooke's law The extension of a spring is directly proportional to the force applied, provided its limit of proportionality is not exceeded.

Hydrated Describes a substance that contains water in its crystals, e.g. hydrated copper sulfate.

I

Impact time Time taken for a collision to take place.

Inert Unreactive.

Insoluble molecules Molecules that will not dissolve in a particular solvent such as water.

Insulating Reducing energy transfer by heating.

Intermolecular force The attraction between the individual molecules in a covalently bonded substance.

Ion A charged particle produced by the loss or gain of electrons.

Ionic bonding The electrostatic force of attraction between positively and negatively charged ions.

Ionisation Any process in which atoms become charged.

Isomerase An enzyme that converts one form of a molecule into another.

Isotope Atom that has the same number of protons but different number of neutrons, i.e. it has the same atomic number but different mass number.

K

Kinetic energy Energy of a moving object due to its motion; kinetic energy (in joules, J) = mass (in kilograms, kg) × (speed)^2 (in m^2/s^2).

L

Lactic acid One product of anaerobic respiration. It builds up in muscles with exercise. Important in yoghurt- and cheese-making processes.

Light energy Energy in the form of light.

Light-dependent resistor Device with a resistance that varies with the amount of light falling on it.

Limit of proportionality The limit for Hooke's law applied to the extension of a stretched spring.

Limiting factor Factor that limits the rate of a reaction, e.g. temperature, pH, light levels (photosynthesis).

Lipase Enzyme that breaks down fats and oils into fatty acids and glycerol.

Lipid Oil or fat.

Live wire The wire of a mains circuit that has a potential that alternates from positive to negative and back each cycle.

M

Macromolecule Giant covalent structure.

Main sequence star The main stage is the life of a star during which it radiates energy because of fusion of hydrogen nuclei in its core.

Mass The quantity of matter in an object; a measure of the difficulty of changing the motion of an object (in kilograms, kg).

Mass number The number of protons plus neutrons in the nucleus of an atom.

Mass spectrometer A machine that can be used to analyse small amounts of a substance to identify it and to find its relative molecular mass.

Mean The arithmetical average of a series of numbers.

Median The middle value in a list of data.

Meiosis The two-stage process of cell division which reduces the chromosome number of the daughter cells. It is involved in making the gametes for sexual reproduction.

Mesophyll tissue The tissue in a green plant where photosynthesis takes place.

Mineral ion Chemical needed in small amounts as part of a balanced diet to keep the body healthy.

Mitochondria The site of aerobic cellular respiration in a cell.

Mitosis Asexual cell division where two identical cells are formed.

Mode The number that occurs most often in a set of data.

Mole The amount of substance in the relative atomic or formula mass of a substance in grams.

Molecular formula The chemical formula that shows the actual numbers of atoms in a particular molecule (e.g. C_2H_4).

Molecular ion peak The peak on the mass spectrum of a substance which tells us the relative molecular mass of the substance. The peak is produced by the heaviest positive ion shown on the mass spectrum.

Momentum This equals mass (in kg) × velocity (in m/s). The unit of momentum is the kilogram metre per second (kg m/s).

Multicellular organism An organism that is made up of many different cells which work together. Some of the cells are specialised for different functions in the organism.

Muscle tissue The tissue that makes up the muscles. It can contract and relax.

N

Nanoscience The study of very tiny particles or structures between 1 and 100 nanometres in size – where 1 nanometre = 10.9 metres.

Net movement The overall movement of …

Neutral A solution with a pH value of 7 that is neither acidic nor an alkaline. Alternatively, something that carries no overall electrical charge – neither positively nor negatively charged.

Neutralisation The chemical reaction of an acid with a base in which they cancel each other out, forming a salt and water. If the base is a carbonate or hydrogen carbonate, carbon dioxide is also produced in the reaction.

Neutral wire The wire of a mains circuit that is earthed at the local substation so its potential is close to zero.

Neutron A dense particle found in the nucleus of an atom. It is electrically neutral, carrying no charge.

Neutron star The highly compressed core of a massive star that remains after a supernova explosion.

Newton The unit of force (N).

Nitrate ion Ion that is needed by plants to make proteins.

Nuclear fission The process in which certain nuclei (uranium-235 and plutonium-239) split into two fragments, releasing energy and two or three neutrons as a result.

Nuclear fusion The process in which small nuclei are forced together so they fuse with each other to form a larger nucleus.

Nucleus (of a cell) An organelle found in many living cells containing the genetic information.

Nucleus (of an atom) The very small and dense central part of an atom, which contains protons and neutrons.

O

Ohm's law The current through a resistor at constant temperature is directly proportional to the potential difference across the resistor.

Ohmic conductor A conductor that has a constant resistance and therefore obeys Ohm's law.

Organ system A group of organs working together to carry out a particular function.

Oscilloscope A device used to display the shape of an electrical wave.

Ova The female sex cells, eggs.

Oxidation The reaction when oxygen is added to a substance (or when electrons are lost).

Oxygen debt The extra oxygen that must be taken into the body after exercise has stopped to complete the aerobic respiration of lactic acid.

P

Parallel Components connected in a circuit so that the potential difference is the same across each one.

Percentage yield The actual mass of product collected in a reaction divided by the maximum mass that could have been formed in theory, multiplied by 100.

Permanent vacuole A space in the cytoplasm filled with cell sap that is there all the time.

pH scale A number that shows how strongly acidic or alkaline a solution is. Acids have a pH value of less than 7 (pH 1 is strongly acidic). Alkalis have a pH value above 7 (pH 14 is strongly alkaline). A neutral liquid has a pH value of 7.

Phloem tissue The living transport tissue in plants that carries sugars around the plant.

Polydactyly A genetic condition inherited through a dominant allele that results in extra fingers and toes.

Potential difference A measure of the work done or energy transferred to the lamp by each coulomb of charge that passes through it. The unit of potential difference is the volt (V).

Power The energy transformed or transferred per second. The unit of power is the watt (W).

Precipitate An insoluble solid formed by a reaction taking place in solution.

Predator Animal that preys on other animals for food.

Protease An enzyme that breaks down proteins.

Protein synthesis The process by which proteins are made on the ribosomes based on information from the genes in the nucleus.

Proton A tiny positive particle found inside the nucleus of an atom.

Protostar The concentration of dust clouds and gas in space that forms a star.

Q

Quadrat A piece of apparatus for sampling organisms in the field.

Quantitative sampling Sampling that records the numbers of organisms rather than just the type.

R

Radioactive dating The use of a radioactive substance to give information about the age of an object.

Range The maximum and minimum values of the independent or dependent variables; important in ensuring that any pattern is detected.

Recessive The characteristic that will show up in the offspring only if both of the alleles are inherited.

Red giant A star that has expanded and cooled, resulting in it becoming red and much larger and cooler than it was before it expanded.

Reduction A reaction in which oxygen is removed (or electrons are gained).

Relative atomic mass, A_r The average mass of the atoms of an element compared with carbon-12 (which is given a mass of exactly 12). The average mass must take into account the proportions of the naturally occurring isotopes of the element.

Relative formula mass, M_r The total of the relative atomic masses, added up in the ratio shown in the chemical formula, of a substance.

Repeatability (of data) We can improve the accuracy of data by repeating measurements and calculating the mean (having retested or discarded any anomalous results).

Repel To cause to move apart.

Reproducibility (of data) The consistency of data that is collected when different people carry out the same investigation.

Residual current circuit breaker (RCCB) An RCCB cuts off the current in the live wire when it is different from the current in the neutral wire.

Resistance Resistance (in ohms, Ω) = potential difference (in volts, V) ÷ current (in amperes, A).

Resultant force The combined effect of the forces acting on an object.

Retention time The time it takes a component in a mixture to pass through the column during gas chromatography.

Reversible reaction A reaction in which the products can re-form the reactants.

Ribosome The site of protein synthesis in a cell.

S

Salivary gland Gland in the mouth that produces saliva containing the enzyme amylase.

Salt A salt is a compound formed when some or all of the hydrogen in an acid is replaced by a metal (or by an ammonium ion). For example, potassium nitrate, KNO_3 (from nitric acid).

Sample size The size of a sample in an investigation.

Series Components connected in a circuit so that the same current that passes through them are in series with each other.

Sex chromosome The chromosome that carries the information about the sex of an individual.

Shape memory alloy Mixture of metals which respond to changes in temperature.

Small intestine The region of the digestive system where most of the digestion of the food takes place.

Socket A mains socket is used to connect the mains plug of a mains appliance to the mains circuit.

Specialised Adapted for a particular function.

Speciation The formation of a new species.

Speed Distance moved ÷ time taken.

Star A large ball of gas in space that emits radiation.

State symbol The abbreviations used in balanced symbol equations to show if reactants and products are solid (s), liquid (l), gas (g) or dissolved in water (aq).

Stem cell Undifferentiated cell with the potential to form a wide variety of different cell types.

Stopping distance Thinking distance + braking distance.

Substrate The material or chemical on which an enzyme acts.

Supergiant A massive star that becomes much larger than a giant star when fusion of helium nuclei commences.

Supernova The explosion of a massive star after fusion in its core ceases and the matter surrounding its core collapses on to the core and rebounds.

T

Terminal velocity The velocity reached by an object when the drag force on it is equal and opposite to the force making it move.

Thermal decomposition The breakdown of a compound by heat.

Thermistor Device with a resistance that varies with temperature.

Thermosetting polymer Polymer that can form extensive cross-linking between chains, resulting in rigid materials which are heat-resistant.

Thermosoftening polymer Polymer that forms plastics which can be softened by heat, then remoulded into different shapes as they cool down and set.

Thinking distance The distance travelled by the vehicle in the time it takes the driver to react.

Three-pin plug A three-pin plug has a live pin, a neutral pin and an earth pin. The earth pin is used to earth the metal case of an appliance so the case cannot become live.

Tracer A small amount of a radioactive substance used to give information about a mechanical or biological system.

Transect A measured line or area along which ecological measurements (e.g. quadrats) are made.

U

Universal indicator A mixture of indicators which can change through a range of colours depending on the pH of a solution. Its colour is matched to a pH number using a pH scale. It shows how strongly acidic or alkaline liquids and solutions are.

V

Valid Suitability of the investigative procedure to answer the question being asked.

Variable – dependent The variable for which the value is measured for each and every change in the independent variable.

Variable – independent The variable for which values are changed or selected by the investigator.

Variable Physical, chemical or biological quantity or characteristic.

Variegated Having different colours, e.g. a green and white leaf.

Velocity Speed in a given direction (in metres/second, m/s).

Volt (V) The unit of potential difference, equal to energy transfer per unit charge in joules per coulomb.

W

Weight The force of gravity on an object (in newtons, N).

White dwarf A star that has collapsed from the red giant stage to become much hotter and denser than it was.

Work Energy transferred by a force, given by: Work done (in joules, J) = force (in newtons, N) × distance moved in the direction of the force (in metres, m).

X

Xylem tissue The non-living transport tissue in plants that transports water around the plant.

Y

Yield See Percentage yield.